THE LAST TEMPLAR

THE KNIGHT IN THE CRYPT

SCRIPT
RAYMOND KHOURY

ARTWORK
MIGUEL LALOR

ASSISTED BY
DANIEL OLIVEIRA

COLOURS
THORN

CINEBOOK
The 9th Art Publisher

Original title: Le Dernier Templier – Le Chevalier de la crypte
Original edition: © Dargaud, 2010 by Khoury & Lalor
www.dargaud.com
All rights reserved
Re-adaptation into English and additional translation: © 2015 Cinebook Ltd
Translator: Mark Bence
Lettering and text layout: Design Amorandi
Printed in Spain by EGEDSA
This edition first published in Great Britain in 2016 by
Cinebook Ltd
56 Beech Avenue
Canterbury, Kent
CT4 7TA
www.cinebook.com
A CIP catalogue record for this book
is available from the British Library
ISBN 978-1-84918-308-6

9th CINEBOOK
The 9th Art Publisher

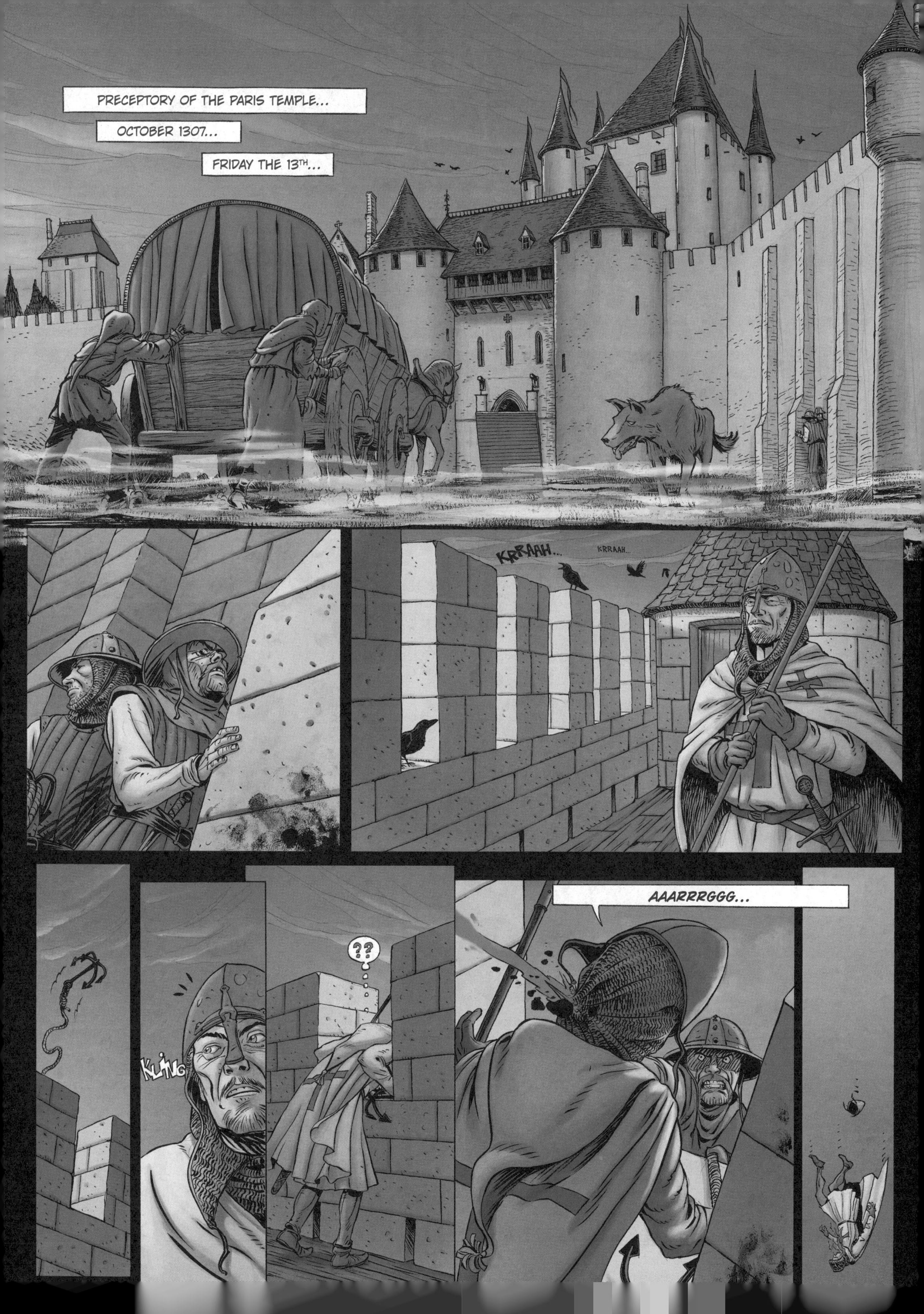

PRECEPTORY OF THE PARIS TEMPLE...
OCTOBER 1307...
FRIDAY THE 13TH...
KRRAAH...
KRRAAH...
KLING
??
AAARRRGGG...

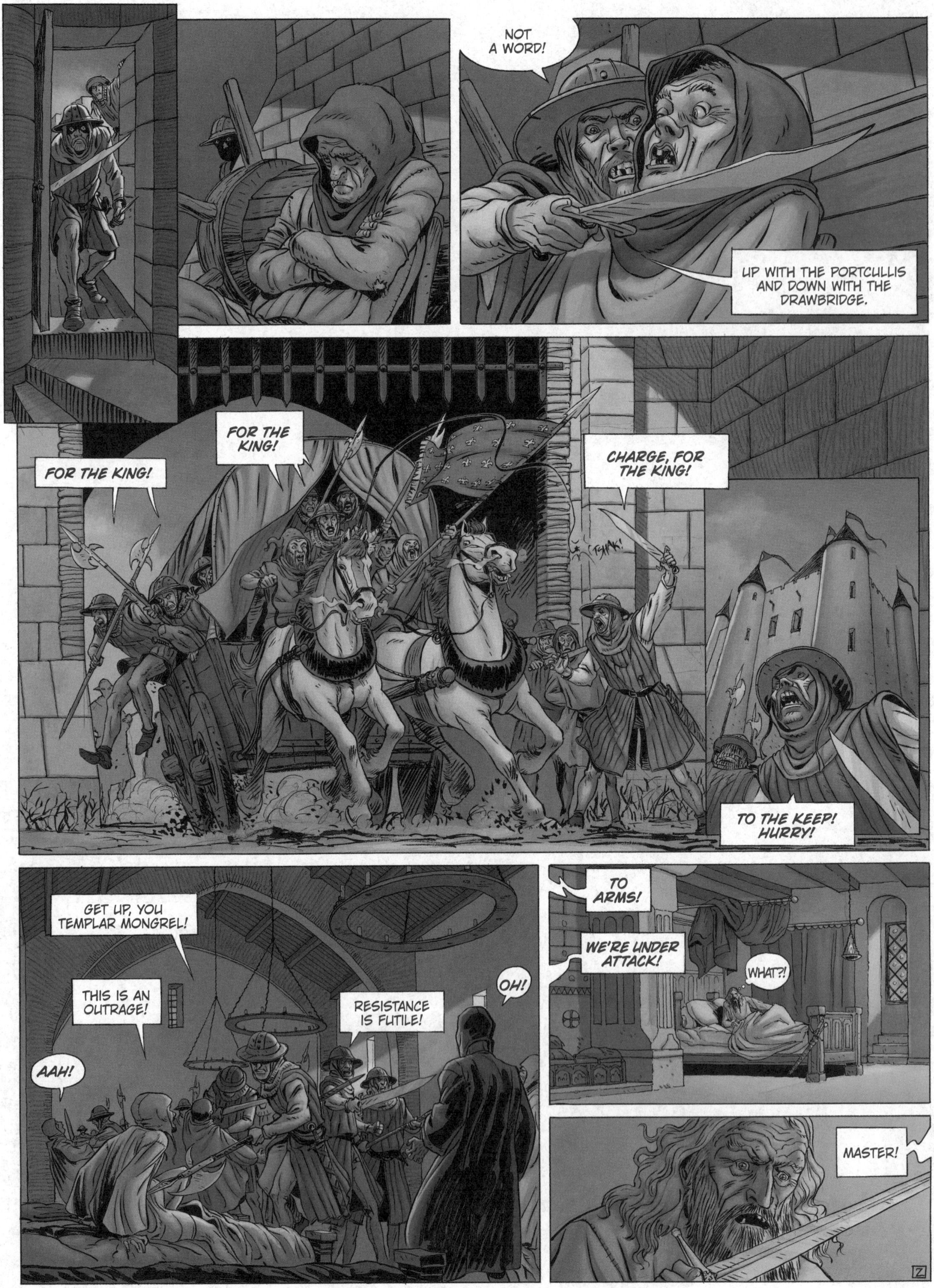
NOT A WORD!
UP WITH THE PORTCULLIS AND DOWN WITH THE DRAWBRIDGE.
FOR THE KING!
FOR THE KING!
CHARGE, FOR THE KING!
TSHAK!
TO THE KEEP! HURRY!
GET UP, YOU TEMPLAR MONGREL!
THIS IS AN OUTRAGE!
AAH!
RESISTANCE IS FUTILE!
OH!
TO ARMS!
WE'RE UNDER ATTACK!
WHAT?!
MASTER!

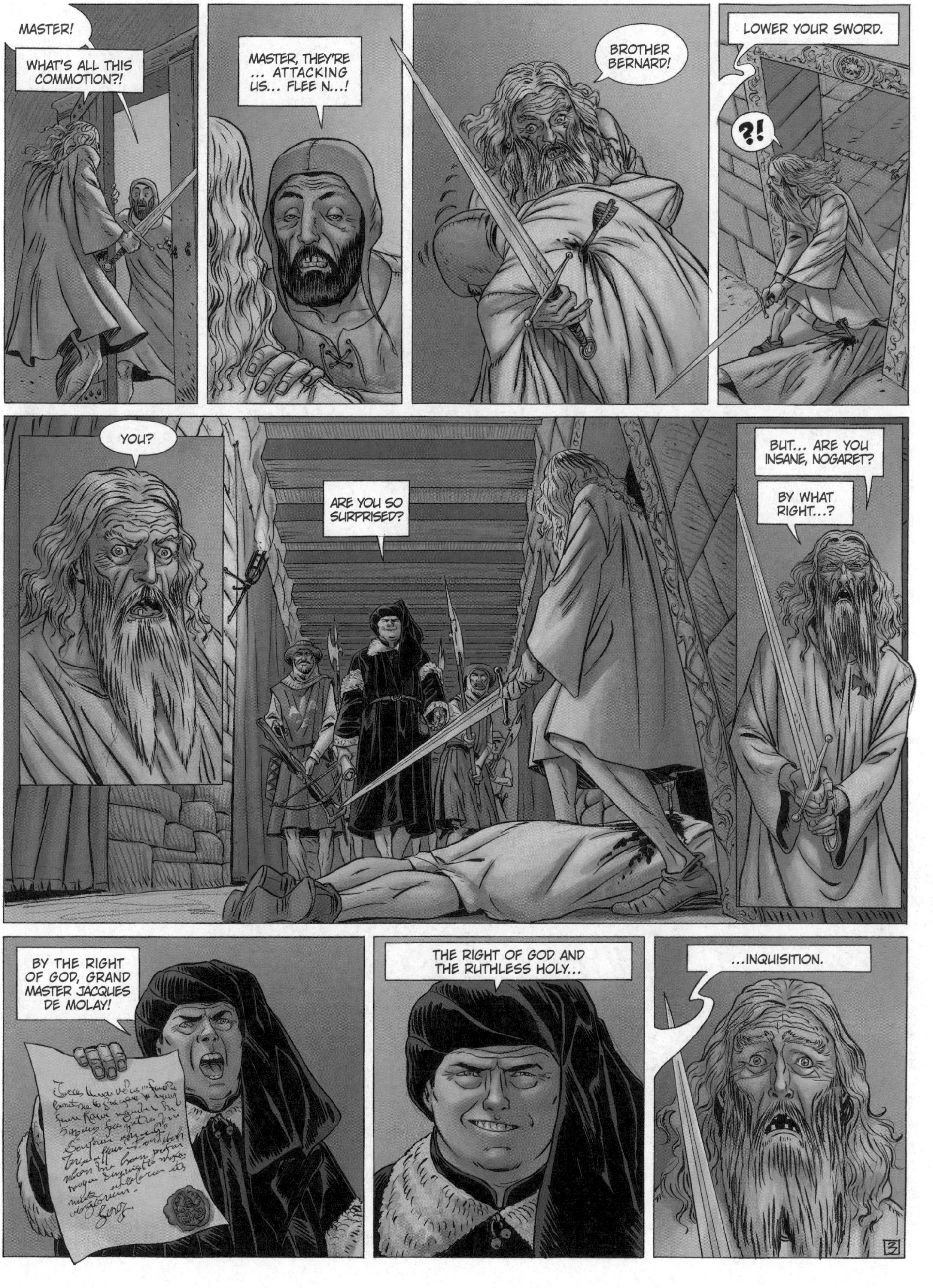
MASTER!
WHAT'S ALL THIS COMMOTION?!
MASTER, THEY'RE ... ATTACKING US... FLEE N...!
BROTHER BERNARD!
LOWER YOUR SWORD.
?!
YOU?
ARE YOU SO SURPRISED?
BUT... ARE YOU INSANE, NOGARET?
BY WHAT RIGHT...?
BY THE RIGHT OF GOD, GRAND MASTER JACQUES DE MOLAY!
THE RIGHT OF GOD AND THE RUTHLESS HOLY...
...INQUISITION.
3

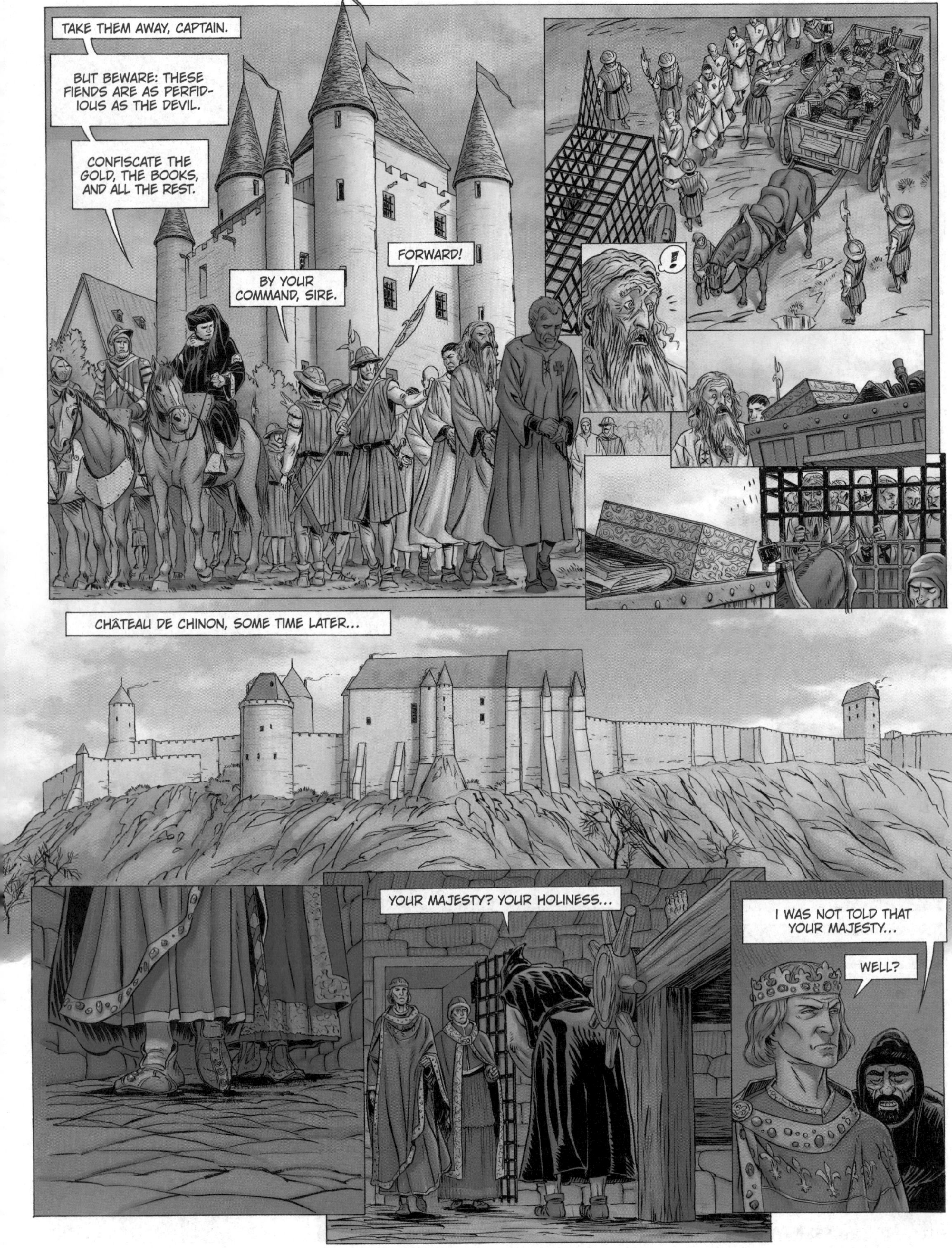
TAKE THEM AWAY, CAPTAIN.
BUT BEWARE: THESE FIENDS ARE AS PERFID-IOUS AS THE DEVIL.
CONFISCATE THE GOLD, THE BOOKS, AND ALL THE REST.
BY YOUR COMMAND, SIRE.
FORWARD!
CHÂTEAU DE CHINON, SOME TIME LATER...
YOUR MAJESTY? YOUR HOLINESS...
I WAS NOT TOLD THAT YOUR MAJESTY...
WELL?

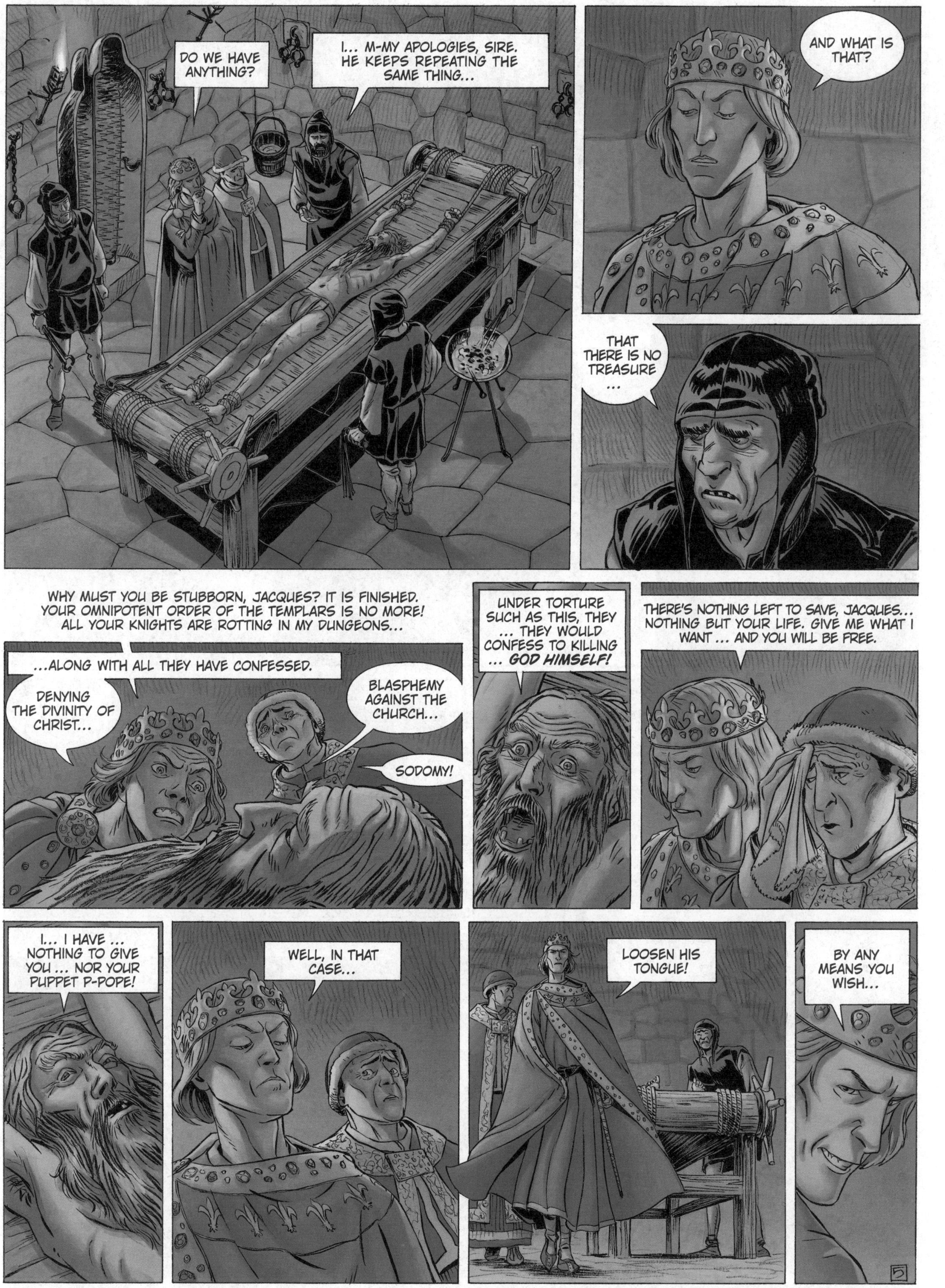
DO WE HAVE ANYTHING?
I... M-MY APOLOGIES, SIRE. HE KEEPS REPEATING THE SAME THING...
AND WHAT IS THAT?
THAT THERE IS NO TREASURE ...
WHY MUST YOU BE STUBBORN, JACQUES? IT IS FINISHED. YOUR OMNIPOTENT ORDER OF THE TEMPLARS IS NO MORE! ALL YOUR KNIGHTS ARE ROTTING IN MY DUNGEONS...
...ALONG WITH ALL THEY HAVE CONFESSED.
DENYING THE DIVINITY OF CHRIST...
BLASPHEMY AGAINST THE CHURCH...
SODOMY!
UNDER TORTURE SUCH AS THIS, THEY ... THEY WOULD CONFESS TO KILLING ... **GOD HIMSELF!**
THERE'S NOTHING LEFT TO SAVE, JACQUES... NOTHING BUT YOUR LIFE. GIVE ME WHAT I WANT ... AND YOU WILL BE FREE.
I... I HAVE ... NOTHING TO GIVE YOU ... NOR YOUR PUPPET P-POPE!
WELL, IN THAT CASE...
LOOSEN HIS TONGUE!
BY ANY MEANS YOU WISH...

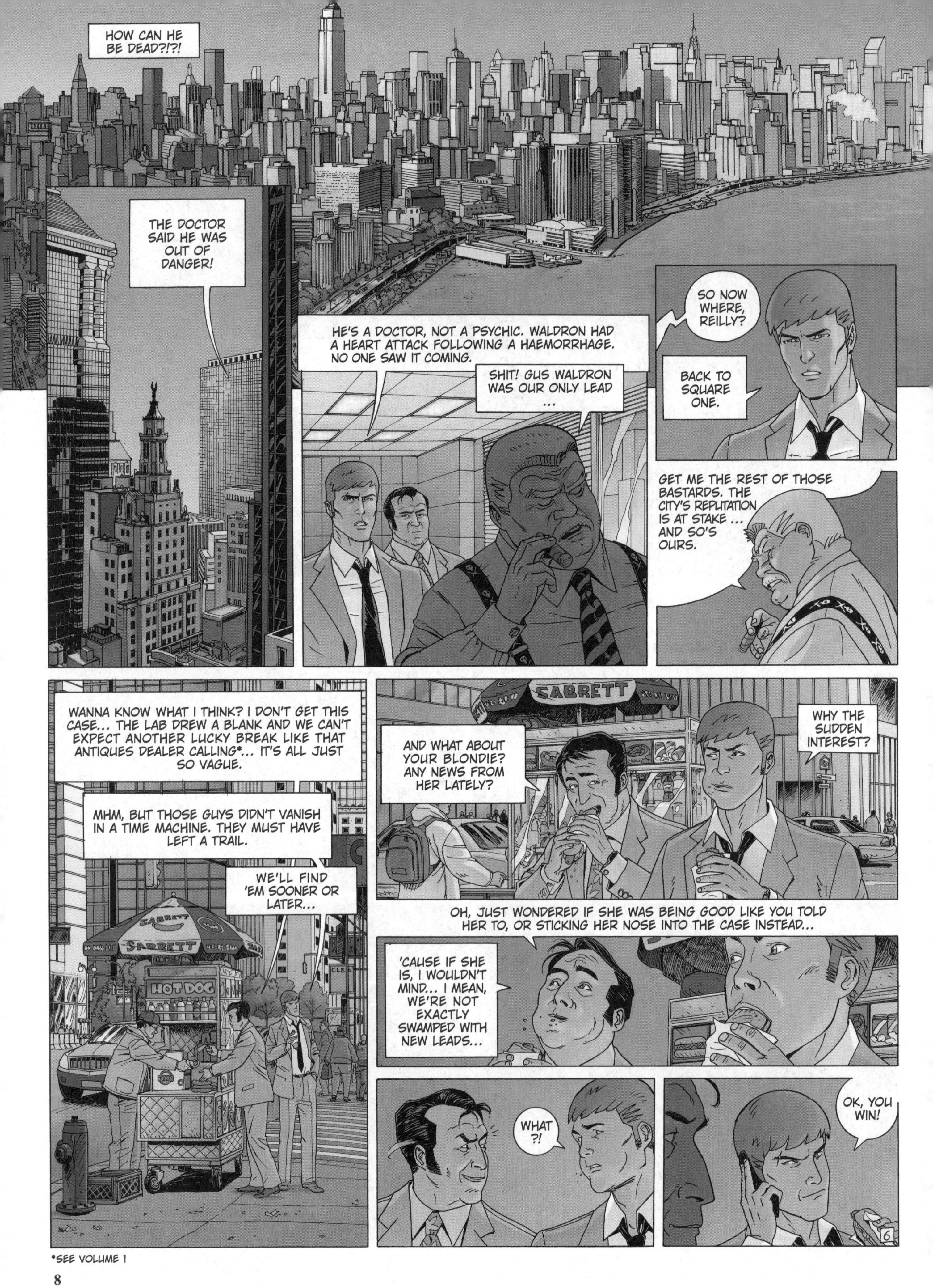
HOW CAN HE BE DEAD?!?!
THE DOCTOR SAID HE WAS OUT OF DANGER!
HE'S A DOCTOR, NOT A PSYCHIC. WALDRON HAD A HEART ATTACK FOLLOWING A HAEMORRHAGE. NO ONE SAW IT COMING.
SHIT! GUS WALDRON WAS OUR ONLY LEAD ...
SO NOW WHERE, REILLY?
BACK TO SQUARE ONE.
GET ME THE REST OF THOSE BASTARDS. THE CITY'S REPUTATION IS AT STAKE ... AND SO'S OURS.
WANNA KNOW WHAT I THINK? I DON'T GET THIS CASE... THE LAB DREW A BLANK AND WE CAN'T EXPECT ANOTHER LUCKY BREAK LIKE THAT ANTIQUES DEALER CALLING*... IT'S ALL JUST SO VAGUE.
MHM, BUT THOSE GUYS DIDN'T VANISH IN A TIME MACHINE. THEY MUST HAVE LEFT A TRAIL.
WE'LL FIND 'EM SOONER OR LATER...
SABRETT
HOT DOG
SABRETT
AND WHAT ABOUT YOUR BLONDIE? ANY NEWS FROM HER LATELY?
WHY THE SUDDEN INTEREST?
OH, JUST WONDERED IF SHE WAS BEING GOOD LIKE YOU TOLD HER TO, OR STICKING HER NOSE INTO THE CASE INSTEAD...
'CAUSE IF SHE IS, I WOULDN'T MIND... I MEAN, WE'RE NOT EXACTLY SWAMPED WITH NEW LEADS...
WHAT ?!
OK, YOU WIN!
6

*SEE VOLUME 1

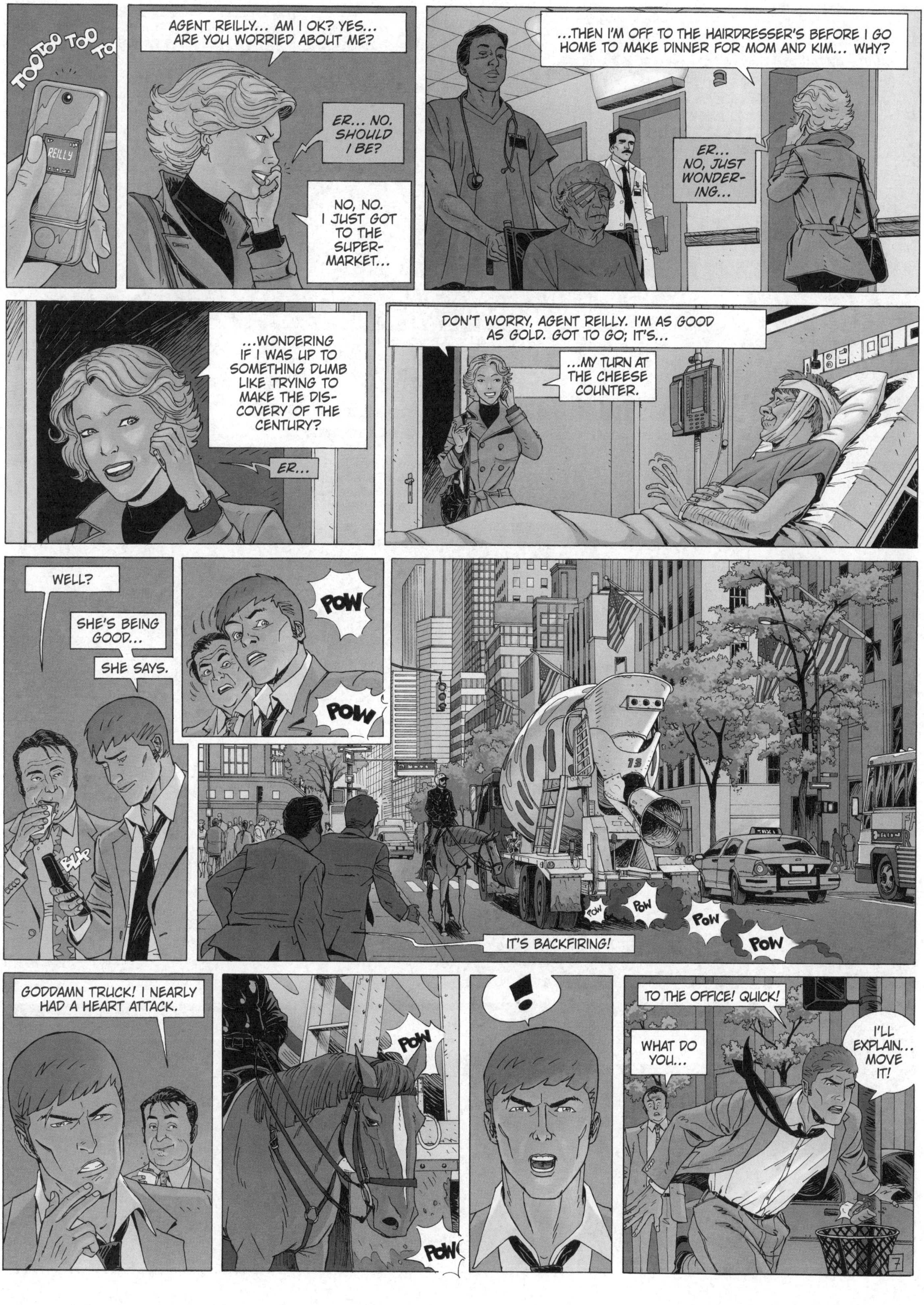
TOOTOO TOO TOO
REILLY
AGENT REILLY... AM I OK? YES... ARE YOU WORRIED ABOUT ME?
ER... NO. SHOULD I BE?
NO, NO. I JUST GOT TO THE SUPER-MARKET...
...THEN I'M OFF TO THE HAIRDRESSER'S BEFORE I GO HOME TO MAKE DINNER FOR MOM AND KIM... WHY?
ER... NO, JUST WONDER-ING...
...WONDERING IF I WAS UP TO SOMETHING DUMB LIKE TRYING TO MAKE THE DIS-COVERY OF THE CENTURY?
ER...
DON'T WORRY, AGENT REILLY. I'M AS GOOD AS GOLD. GOT TO GO; IT'S...
...MY TURN AT THE CHEESE COUNTER.
WELL?
SHE'S BEING GOOD...
SHE SAYS.
BLIP
POW
POW
POW
POW
POW
POW
IT'S BACKFIRING!
GODDAMN TRUCK! I NEARLY HAD A HEART ATTACK.
POW
POW
!
TO THE OFFICE! QUICK!
WHAT DO YOU...
I'LL EXPLAIN... MOVE IT!

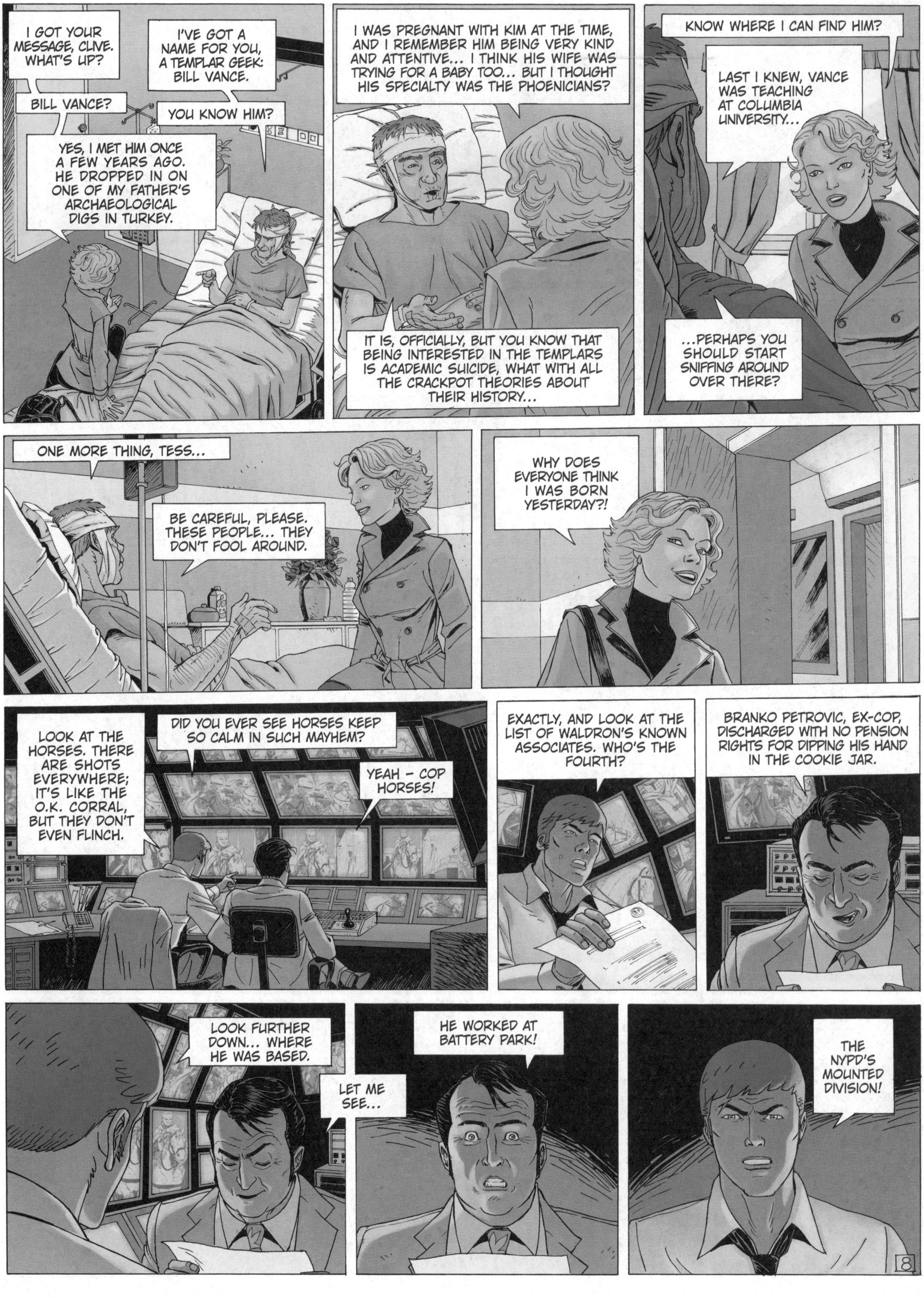
I GOT YOUR MESSAGE, CLIVE. WHAT'S UP?
I'VE GOT A NAME FOR YOU, A TEMPLAR GEEK: BILL VANCE.
BILL VANCE?
YOU KNOW HIM?
YES, I MET HIM ONCE A FEW YEARS AGO. HE DROPPED IN ON ONE OF MY FATHER'S ARCHAEOLOGICAL DIGS IN TURKEY.
I WAS PREGNANT WITH KIM AT THE TIME, AND I REMEMBER HIM BEING VERY KIND AND ATTENTIVE... I THINK HIS WIFE WAS TRYING FOR A BABY TOO... BUT I THOUGHT HIS SPECIALTY WAS THE PHOENICIANS?
IT IS, OFFICIALLY, BUT YOU KNOW THAT BEING INTERESTED IN THE TEMPLARS IS ACADEMIC SUICIDE, WHAT WITH ALL THE CRACKPOT THEORIES ABOUT THEIR HISTORY...
KNOW WHERE I CAN FIND HIM?
LAST I KNEW, VANCE WAS TEACHING AT COLUMBIA UNIVERSITY...
...PERHAPS YOU SHOULD START SNIFFING AROUND OVER THERE?
ONE MORE THING, TESS...
BE CAREFUL, PLEASE. THESE PEOPLE... THEY DON'T FOOL AROUND.
WHY DOES EVERYONE THINK I WAS BORN YESTERDAY?!
LOOK AT THE HORSES. THERE ARE SHOTS EVERYWHERE; IT'S LIKE THE O.K. CORRAL, BUT THEY DON'T EVEN FLINCH.
DID YOU EVER SEE HORSES KEEP SO CALM IN SUCH MAYHEM?
YEAH – COP HORSES!
EXACTLY, AND LOOK AT THE LIST OF WALDRON'S KNOWN ASSOCIATES. WHO'S THE FOURTH?
BRANKO PETROVIC, EX-COP, DISCHARGED WITH NO PENSION RIGHTS FOR DIPPING HIS HAND IN THE COOKIE JAR.
LOOK FURTHER DOWN... WHERE HE WAS BASED.
LET ME SEE...
HE WORKED AT BATTERY PARK!
THE NYPD'S MOUNTED DIVISION!
8

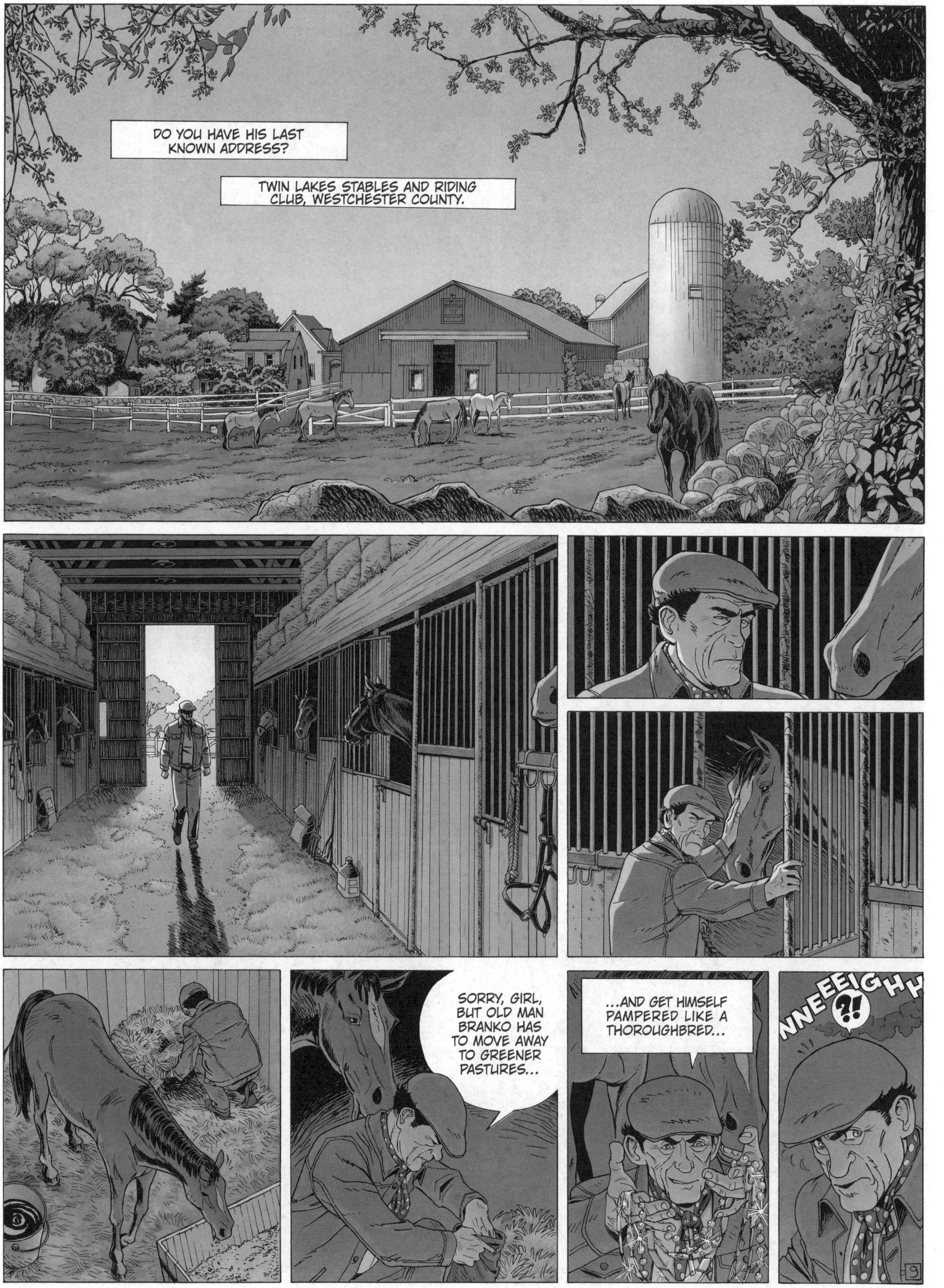
DO YOU HAVE HIS LAST KNOWN ADDRESS?
TWIN LAKES STABLES AND RIDING CLUB, WESTCHESTER COUNTY.
SORRY, GIRL, BUT OLD MAN BRANKO HAS TO MOVE AWAY TO GREENER PASTURES...
...AND GET HIMSELF PAMPERED LIKE A THOROUGHBRED...
NNEEEIGHH
?!

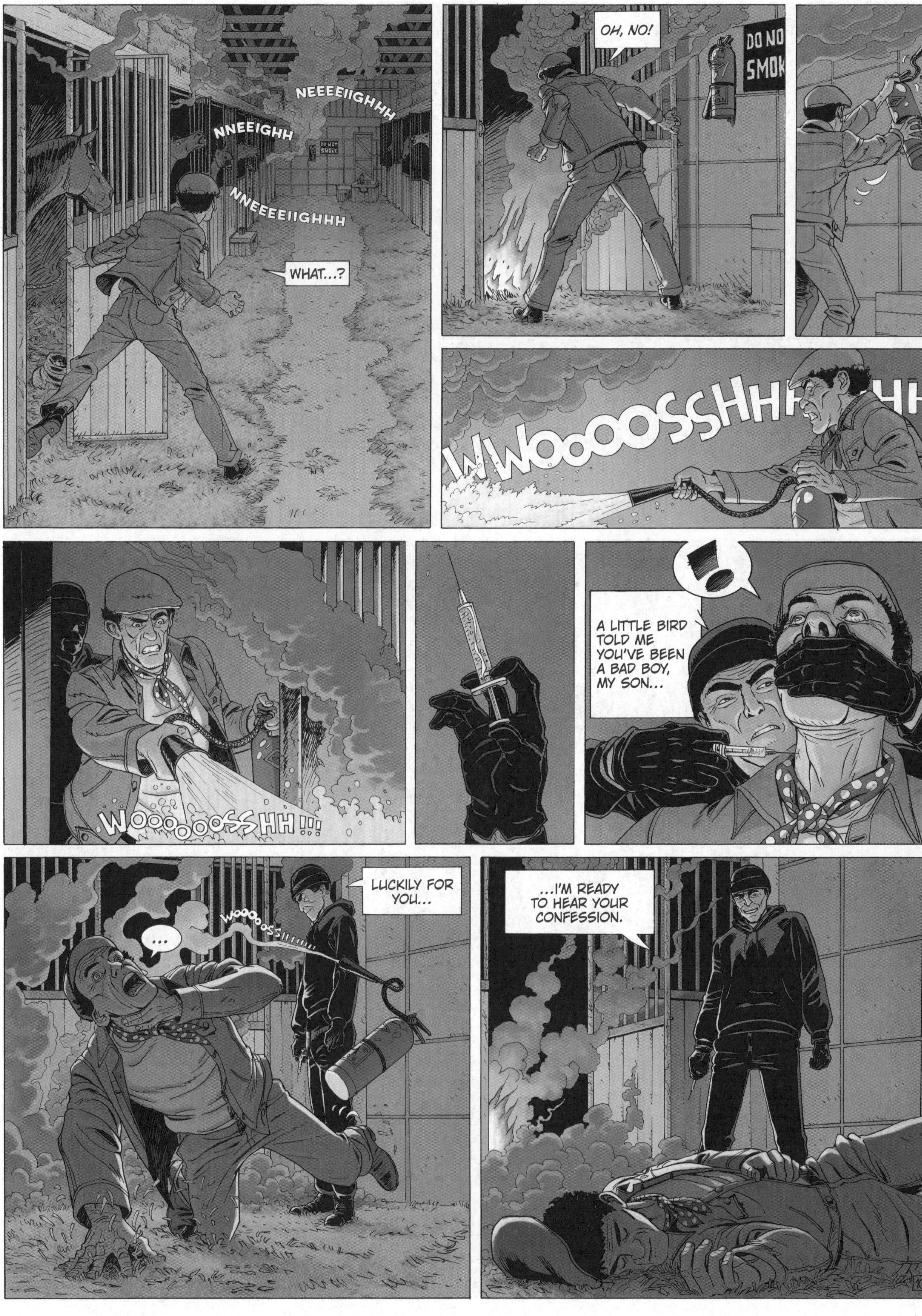

NEEEEIIGHHH
NNEEIGHH
NNEEEEIIGHHH
WHAT...?
OH, NO!
DO NO
SMOK
WWOOOOSSHHHHH
WOOOOOOSSHH!!!
A LITTLE BIRD TOLD ME YOU'VE BEEN A BAD BOY, MY SON...
LUCKILY FOR YOU...
...
WOOOOOSS!!!!
...I'M READY TO HEAR YOUR CONFESSION.
10

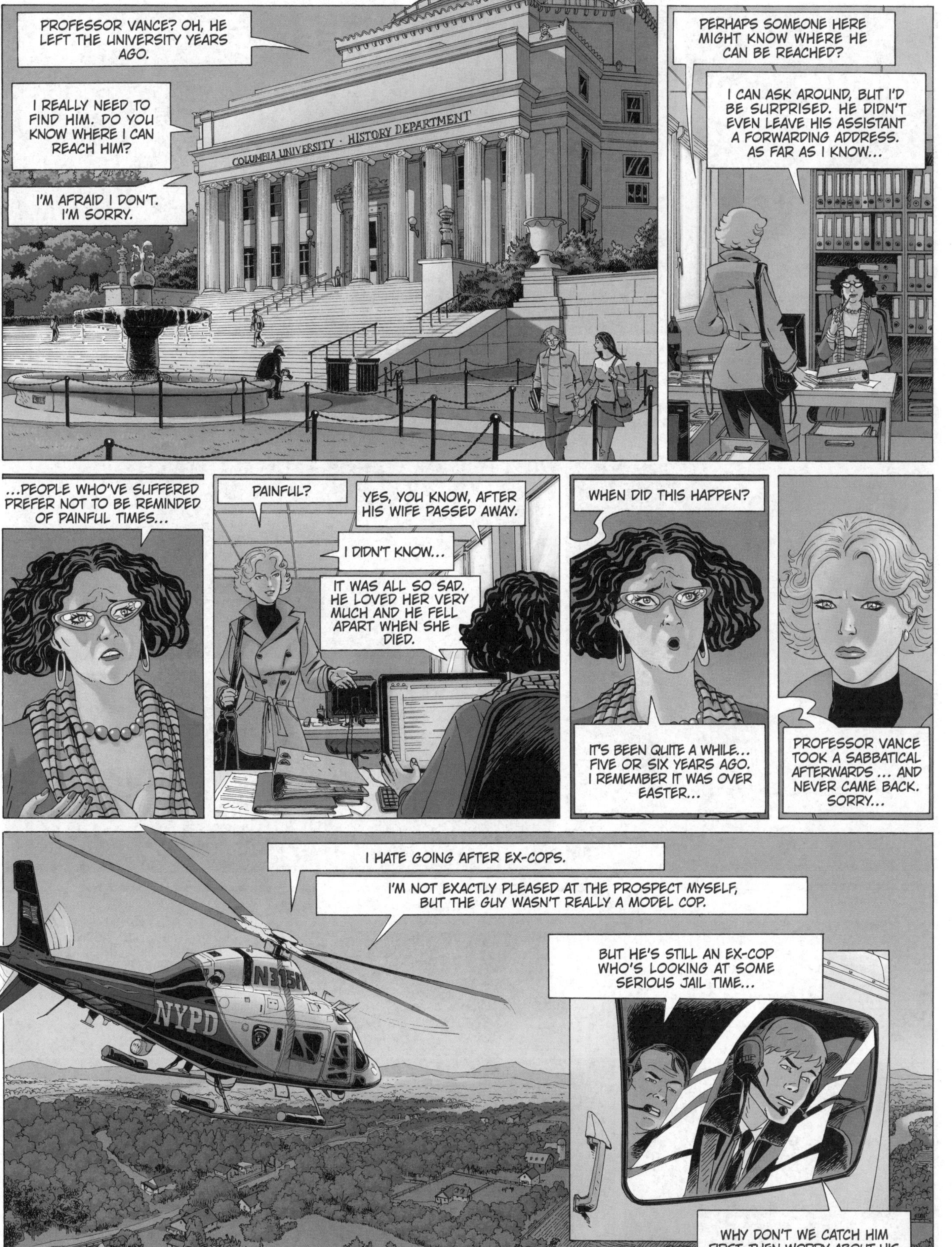
PROFESSOR VANCE? OH, HE LEFT THE UNIVERSITY YEARS AGO.
I REALLY NEED TO FIND HIM. DO YOU KNOW WHERE I CAN REACH HIM?
I'M AFRAID I DON'T. I'M SORRY.
COLUMBIA UNIVERSITY · HISTORY DEPARTMENT
PERHAPS SOMEONE HERE MIGHT KNOW WHERE HE CAN BE REACHED?
I CAN ASK AROUND, BUT I'D BE SURPRISED. HE DIDN'T EVEN LEAVE HIS ASSISTANT A FORWARDING ADDRESS. AS FAR AS I KNOW...
...PEOPLE WHO'VE SUFFERED PREFER NOT TO BE REMINDED OF PAINFUL TIMES...
PAINFUL?
YES, YOU KNOW, AFTER HIS WIFE PASSED AWAY.
I DIDN'T KNOW...
IT WAS ALL SO SAD. HE LOVED HER VERY MUCH AND HE FELL APART WHEN SHE DIED.
WHEN DID THIS HAPPEN?
IT'S BEEN QUITE A WHILE... FIVE OR SIX YEARS AGO. I REMEMBER IT WAS OVER EASTER...
PROFESSOR VANCE TOOK A SABBATICAL AFTERWARDS ... AND NEVER CAME BACK. SORRY...
I HATE GOING AFTER EX-COPS.
I'M NOT EXACTLY PLEASED AT THE PROSPECT MYSELF, BUT THE GUY WASN'T REALLY A MODEL COP.
NYPD
BUT HE'S STILL AN EX-COP WHO'S LOOKING AT SOME SERIOUS JAIL TIME...
WHY DON'T WE CATCH HIM FIRST, THEN WORRY ABOUT HIS SOCIAL WELL-BEING IN JAIL?
11

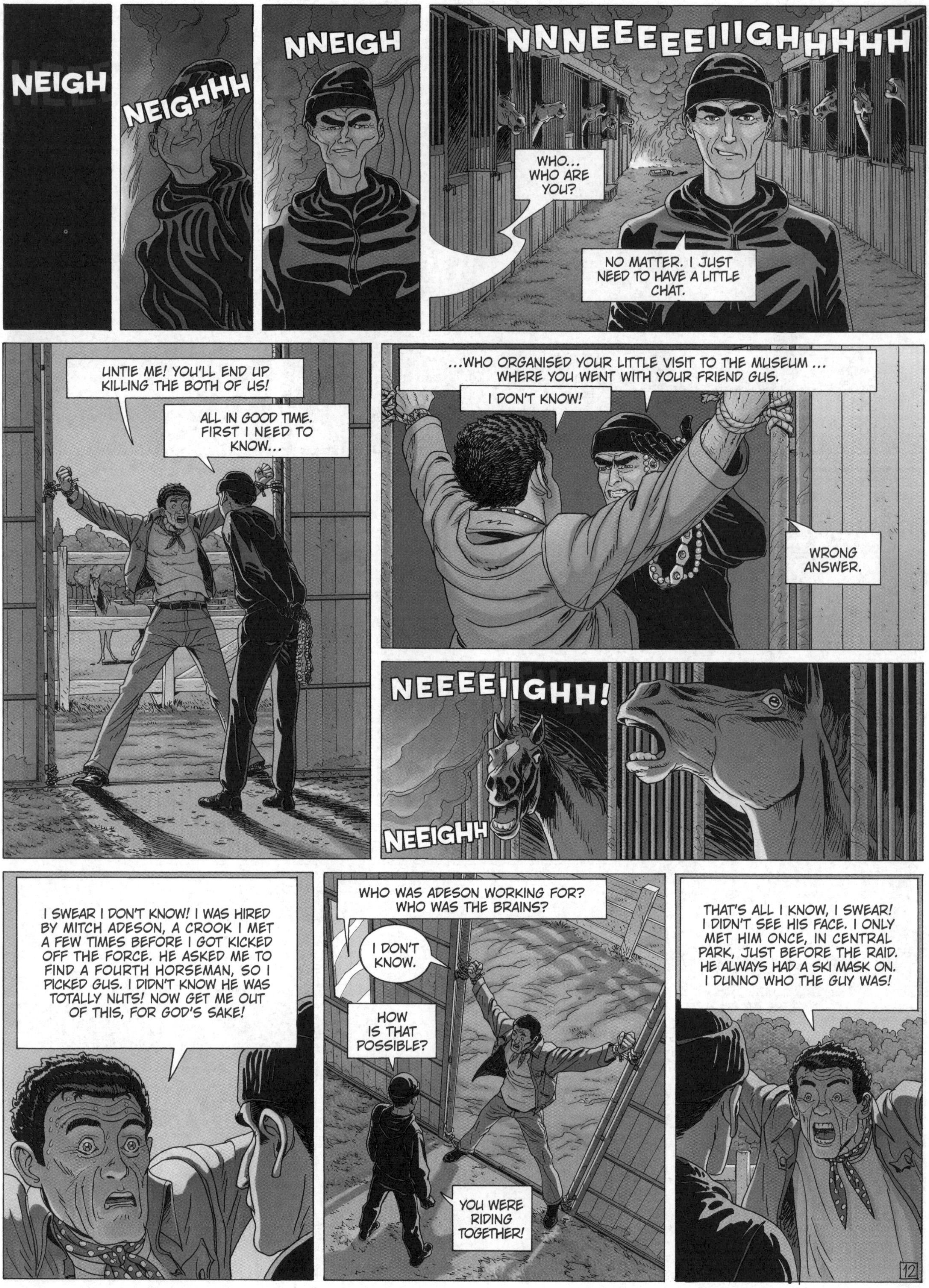
NEIGH
NEIGHHH
NNEIGH
NNNEEEEEEIIIGHHHHH
WHO... WHO ARE YOU?
NO MATTER. I JUST NEED TO HAVE A LITTLE CHAT.
UNTIE ME! YOU'LL END UP KILLING THE BOTH OF US!
ALL IN GOOD TIME. FIRST I NEED TO KNOW...
...WHO ORGANISED YOUR LITTLE VISIT TO THE MUSEUM ... WHERE YOU WENT WITH YOUR FRIEND GUS.
I DON'T KNOW!
WRONG ANSWER.
NEEEEIIGHH!
NEEIGHH
I SWEAR I DON'T KNOW! I WAS HIRED BY MITCH ADESON, A CROOK I MET A FEW TIMES BEFORE I GOT KICKED OFF THE FORCE. HE ASKED ME TO FIND A FOURTH HORSEMAN, SO I PICKED GUS. I DIDN'T KNOW HE WAS TOTALLY NUTS! NOW GET ME OUT OF THIS, FOR GOD'S SAKE!
WHO WAS ADESON WORKING FOR? WHO WAS THE BRAINS?
I DON'T KNOW.
HOW IS THAT POSSIBLE?
YOU WERE RIDING TOGETHER!
THAT'S ALL I KNOW, I SWEAR! I DIDN'T SEE HIS FACE. I ONLY MET HIM ONCE, IN CENTRAL PARK, JUST BEFORE THE RAID. HE ALWAYS HAD A SKI MASK ON. I DUNNO WHO THE GUY WAS!
12

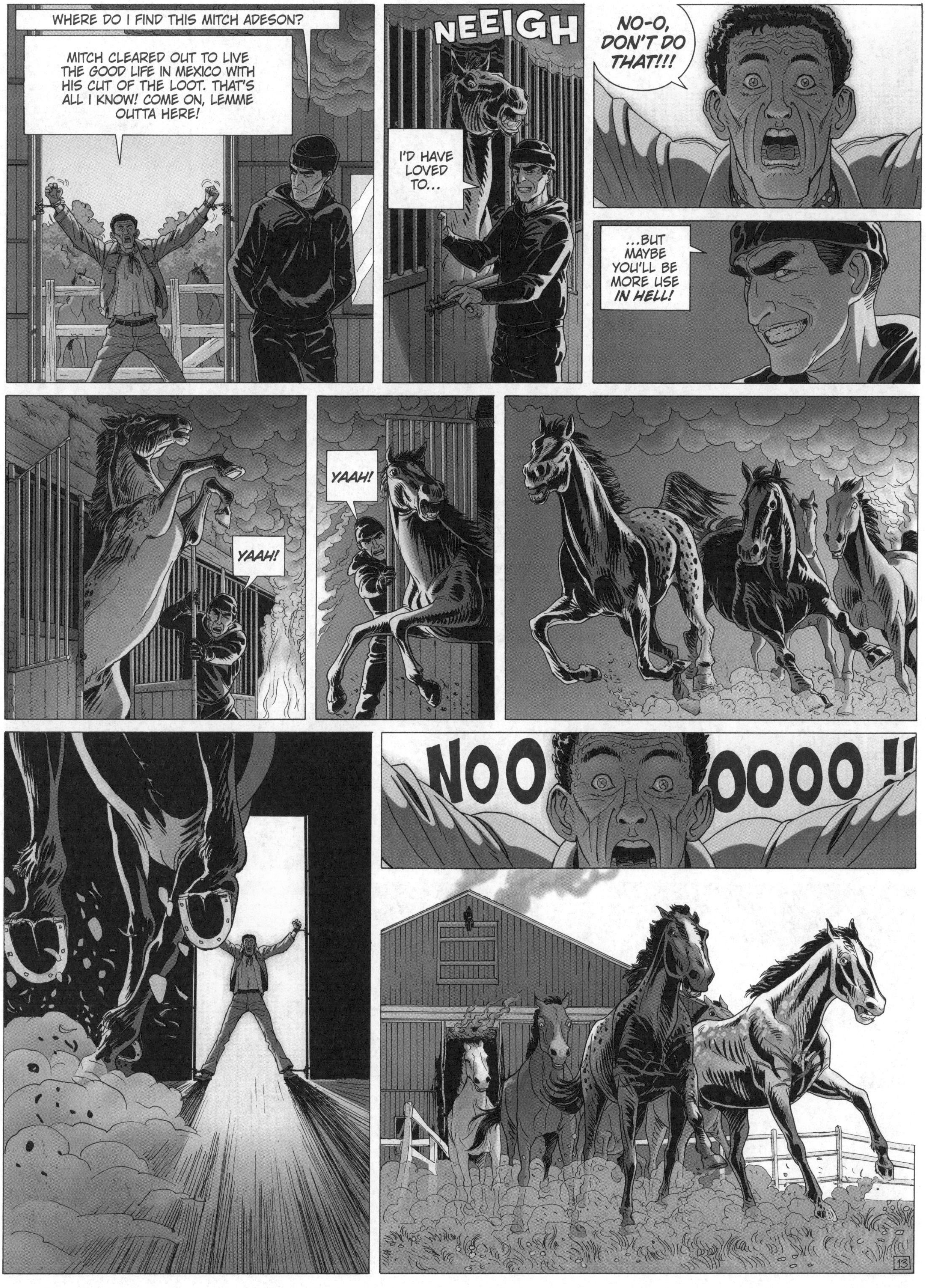
WHERE DO I FIND THIS MITCH ADESON?
MITCH CLEARED OUT TO LIVE THE GOOD LIFE IN MEXICO WITH HIS CUT OF THE LOOT. THAT'S ALL I KNOW! COME ON, LEMME OUTTA HERE!
NEEIGH
I'D HAVE LOVED TO...
NO-O, DON'T DO THAT!!!
...BUT MAYBE YOU'LL BE MORE USE IN HELL!
YAAH!
YAAH!
NOOOOOO !!
13

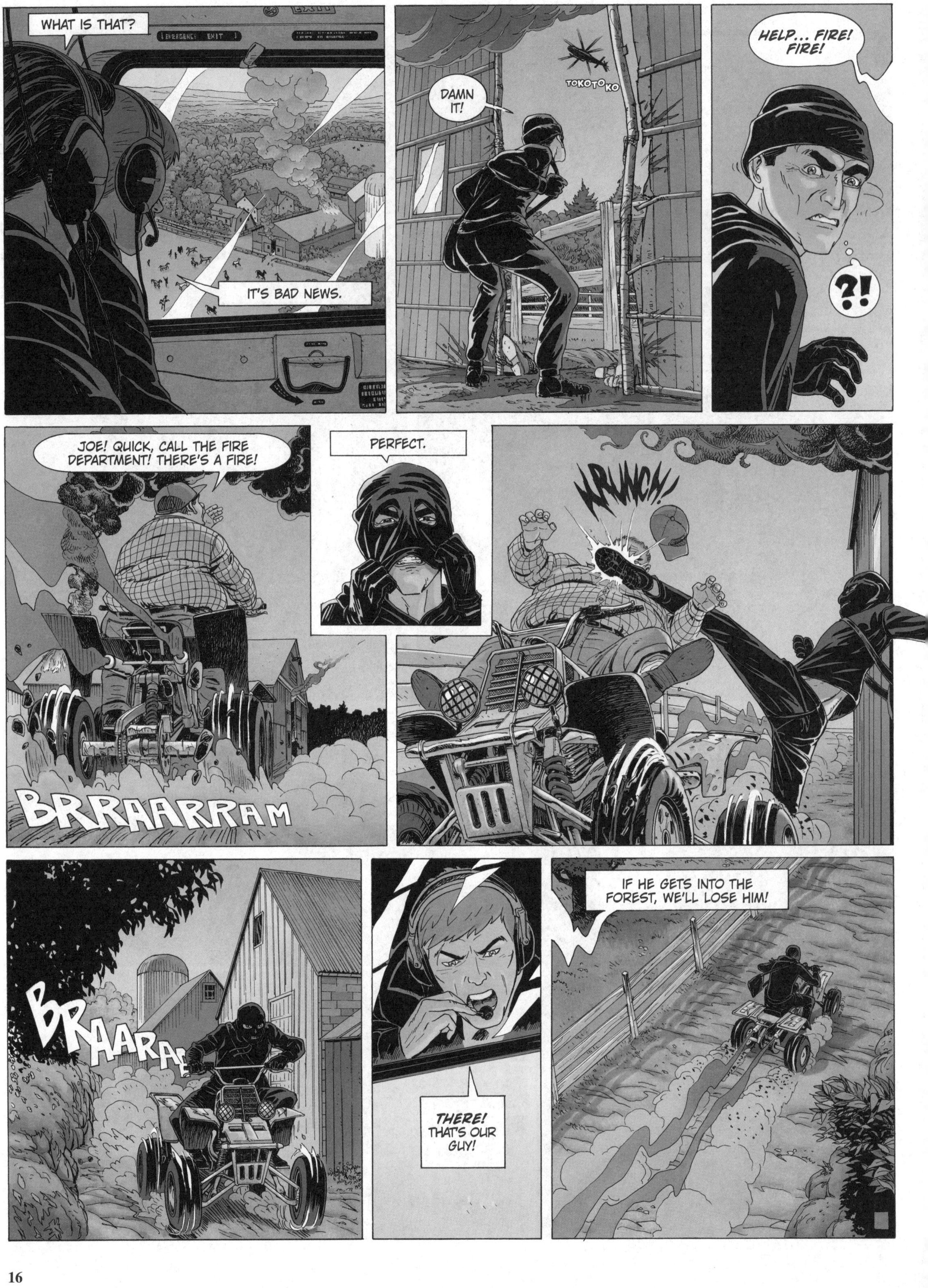
WHAT IS THAT?
IT'S BAD NEWS.
DAMN IT!
TOKOTOKO
HELP... FIRE! FIRE!
?!
JOE! QUICK, CALL THE FIRE DEPARTMENT! THERE'S A FIRE!
BRRAARRRAM
PERFECT.
KRUNCH!
BRAARAE
THERE! THAT'S OUR GUY!
IF HE GETS INTO THE FOREST, WE'LL LOSE HIM!

QUICK! LAND IN FRONT OF THE STABLES!

NEGATIVE! THAT FIELD'S FULL OF TERRIFIED HORSES. THERE'S ANOTHER SPOT TO THE RIGHT...

IT'S TOO FAR! HE'LL BE IN NEW JERSEY BY THEN!

HERE!

DROP DOWN A LITTLE!

NO CAN DO. MY BLADES MIGHT HIT THE SILO.

THEN HOVER RIGHT ABOVE THOSE HAY BALES!

A LITTLE BIT MORE.

!

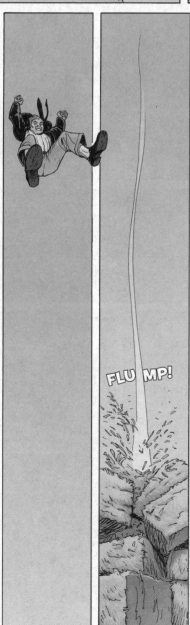

FLU MP!

YOU OK?

YEAH ... BUT I WOULDN'T MAKE A HABIT OF IT...

WHERE DOES THIS TRACK GO?

SEVERAL PLACES... IT'S A HUGE FOREST.

WHOA! EASY NOW!

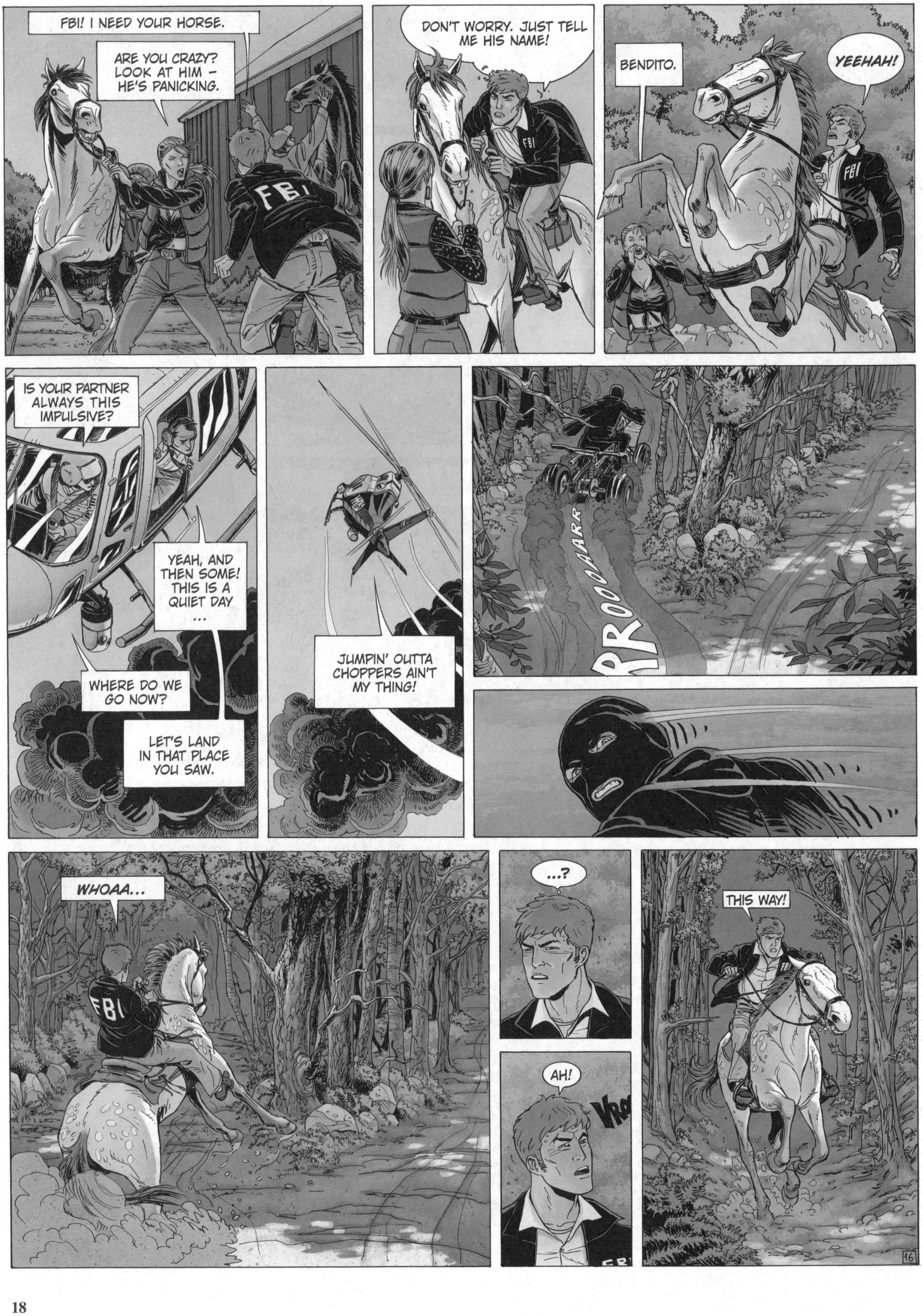

FBI! I NEED YOUR HORSE.
ARE YOU CRAZY? LOOK AT HIM – HE'S PANICKING.
DON'T WORRY. JUST TELL ME HIS NAME!
BENDITO.
YEEHAH!
IS YOUR PARTNER ALWAYS THIS IMPULSIVE?
YEAH, AND THEN SOME! THIS IS A QUIET DAY …
WHERE DO WE GO NOW?
LET'S LAND IN THAT PLACE YOU SAW.
JUMPIN' OUTTA CHOPPERS AIN'T MY THING!
RROOOOAARR
WHOAA…
…?
AH!
THIS WAY!
16

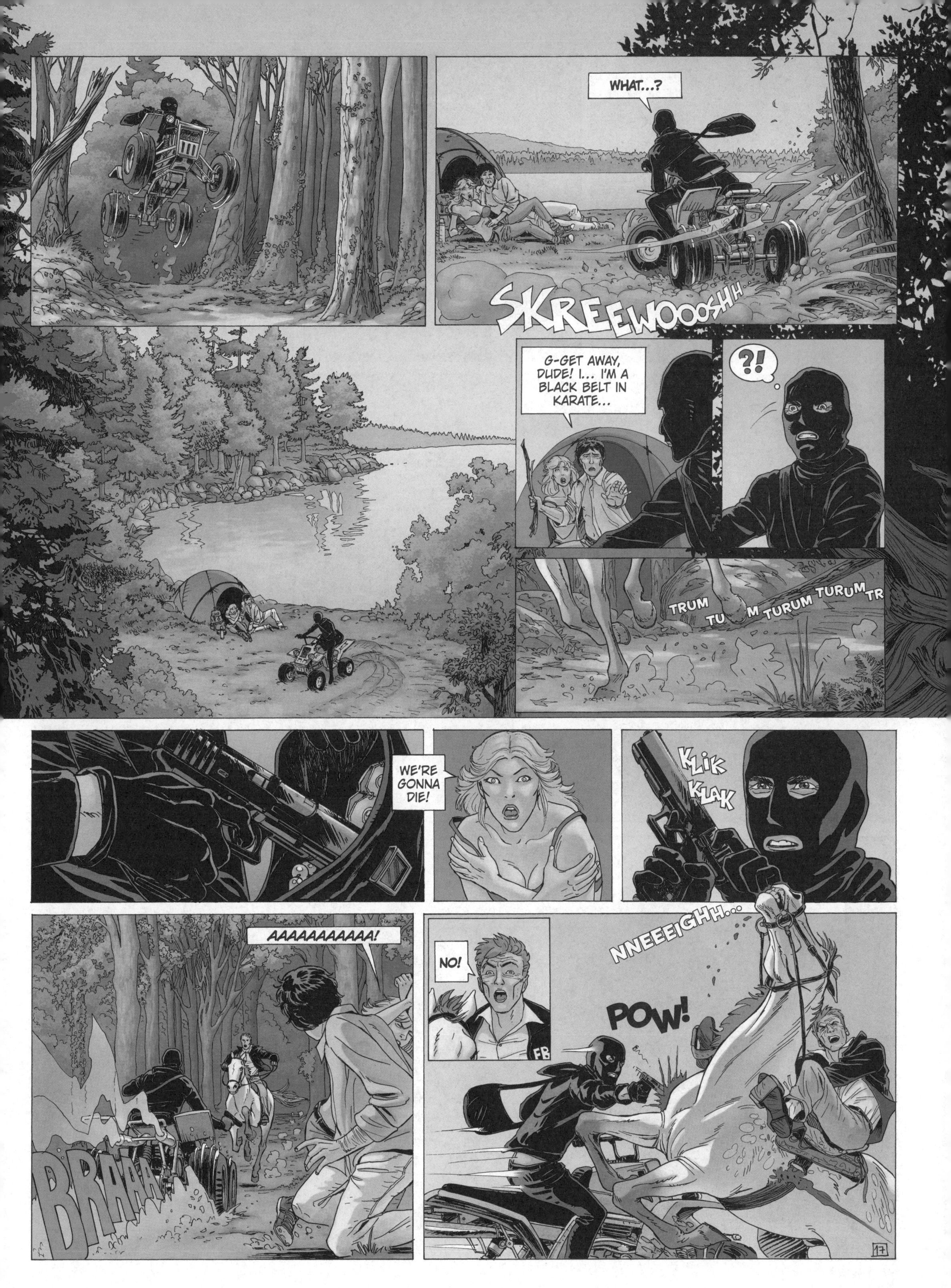

WHAT...?
SKREEWOOOSHH
G-GET AWAY, DUDE! I... I'M A BLACK BELT IN KARATE...
?!
TRUM TUM TURUM TURUM TR
WE'RE GONNA DIE!
KLIK KLAK
AAAAAAAAAAA!
BRAAA
NO!
FB
NNEEEIGHH...
POW!
17

AH!

BRKAAAM

I'M SORRY, BENDITO. I NEVER WANTED THIS.

ARE YOU HURT?

REILLY!

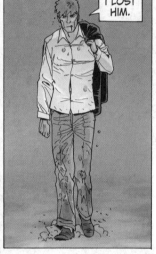

I LOST HIM.

I GUESS THAT'S BRANKO?

YEAH, OR WHAT'S LEFT OF HIM. HE WAS CRUCIFIED ACROSS THE DOORWAY...

THE HORSES LITERALLY STAMPEDED THROUGH HIM... THE FIRE TOOK CARE OF THE REST. WHOEVER DID THIS WAS A REAL SADIST. THAT'S TWO DOWN AND TWO TO GO...

OR JUST ONE, IF THE FOUR HORSEMEN'S BOSS IS BENT ON TAKING OUT HIS ACCOMPLICES...

WE'RE GONNA NEED THE CORONERS TO DO ANOTHER AUTOPSY ON GUS*. I DON'T BELIEVE HIS HEART FAILURE WAS NATURAL.

I BET SOMEONE FAILED IT FOR HIM.

18

*SEE VOLUME 1

20

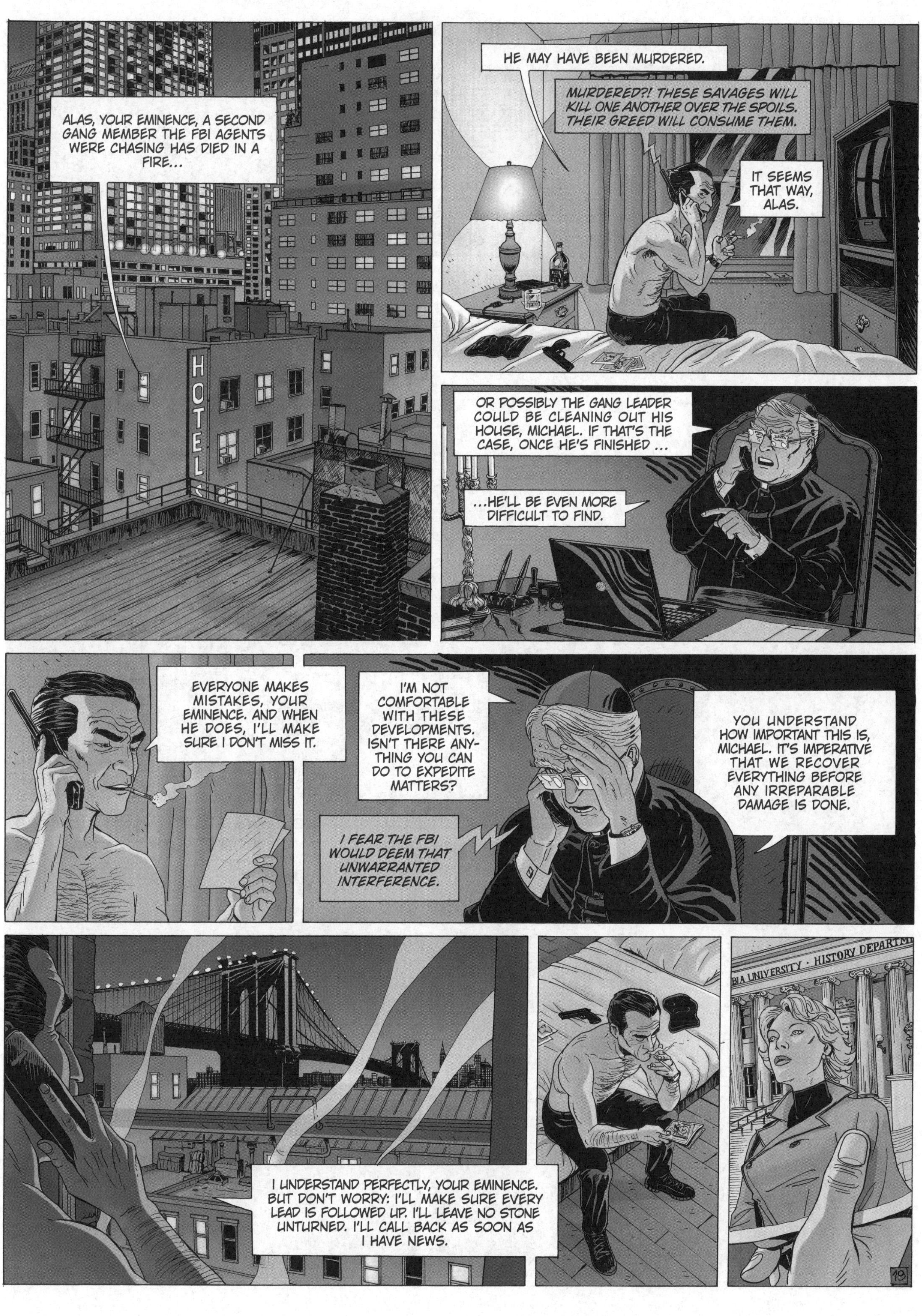

ALAS, YOUR EMINENCE, A SECOND GANG MEMBER THE FBI AGENTS WERE CHASING HAS DIED IN A FIRE...
HOTEL
HE MAY HAVE BEEN MURDERED.
MURDERED?! THESE SAVAGES WILL KILL ONE ANOTHER OVER THE SPOILS. THEIR GREED WILL CONSUME THEM.
IT SEEMS THAT WAY, ALAS.
OR POSSIBLY THE GANG LEADER COULD BE CLEANING OUT HIS HOUSE, MICHAEL. IF THAT'S THE CASE, ONCE HE'S FINISHED ...
...HE'LL BE EVEN MORE DIFFICULT TO FIND.
EVERYONE MAKES MISTAKES, YOUR EMINENCE. AND WHEN HE DOES, I'LL MAKE SURE I DON'T MISS IT.
I'M NOT COMFORTABLE WITH THESE DEVELOPMENTS. ISN'T THERE ANY-THING YOU CAN DO TO EXPEDITE MATTERS?
I FEAR THE FBI WOULD DEEM THAT UNWARRANTED INTERFERENCE.
YOU UNDERSTAND HOW IMPORTANT THIS IS, MICHAEL. IT'S IMPERATIVE THAT WE RECOVER EVERYTHING BEFORE ANY IRREPARABLE DAMAGE IS DONE.
I UNDERSTAND PERFECTLY, YOUR EMINENCE. BUT DON'T WORRY: I'LL MAKE SURE EVERY LEAD IS FOLLOWED UP. I'LL LEAVE NO STONE UNTURNED. I'LL CALL BACK AS SOON AS I HAVE NEWS.
BIA UNIVERSITY · HISTORY DEPARTM
19

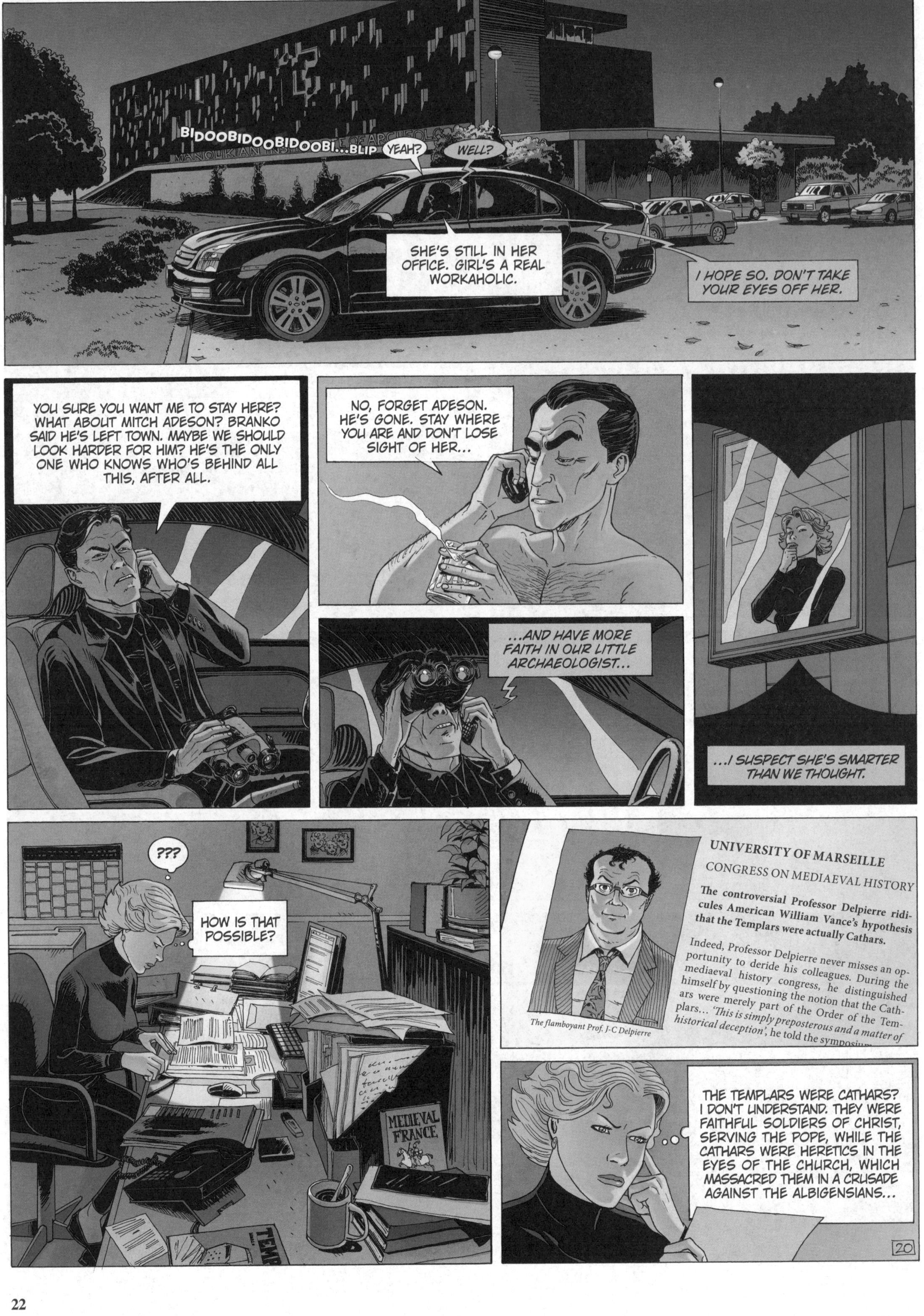

BIDOOBIDOOBIDOOBI...BLIP
YEAH?
WELL?
SHE'S STILL IN HER OFFICE. GIRL'S A REAL WORKAHOLIC.
I HOPE SO. DON'T TAKE YOUR EYES OFF HER.
YOU SURE YOU WANT ME TO STAY HERE? WHAT ABOUT MITCH ADESON? BRANKO SAID HE'S LEFT TOWN. MAYBE WE SHOULD LOOK HARDER FOR HIM? HE'S THE ONLY ONE WHO KNOWS WHO'S BEHIND ALL THIS, AFTER ALL.
NO, FORGET ADESON. HE'S GONE. STAY WHERE YOU ARE AND DON'T LOSE SIGHT OF HER...
...AND HAVE MORE FAITH IN OUR LITTLE ARCHAEOLOGIST...
...I SUSPECT SHE'S SMARTER THAN WE THOUGHT.
???
HOW IS THAT POSSIBLE?
MEDIEVAL FRANCE
UNIVERSITY OF MARSEILLE
CONGRESS ON MEDIAEVAL HISTORY
The controversial Professor Delpierre ridicules American William Vance's hypothesis that the Templars were actually Cathars.
Indeed, Professor Delpierre never misses an opportunity to deride his colleagues. During the mediaeval history congress, he distinguished himself by questioning the notion that the Cathars were merely part of the Order of the Templars... 'This is simply preposterous and a matter of historical deception', he told the symposium
The flamboyant Prof. J-C Delpierre
THE TEMPLARS WERE CATHARS? I DON'T UNDERSTAND. THEY WERE FAITHFUL SOLDIERS OF CHRIST, SERVING THE POPE, WHILE THE CATHARS WERE HERETICS IN THE EYES OF THE CHURCH, WHICH MASSACRED THEM IN A CRUSADE AGAINST THE ALBIGENSIANS...
20

YAAWN...

OK, HALF AN HOUR MORE AND I'LL LEAVE.

WHAT'S THIS?

Professor W. Vance

Martha Vance

PROFESSOR WILLIAM VANCE'S WIFE DIES TRAGICALLY IN CHILDBIRTH

HOW AWFUL! WHAT A TRAGEDY... NO WONDER HE LOST THE DESIRE TO TEACH...

WHAT...?

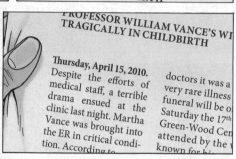

PROFESSOR WILLIAM VANCE'S WI TRAGICALLY IN CHILDBIRTH

Thursday, April 15, 2010. Despite the efforts of medical staff, a terrible drama ensued at the clinic last night. Martha Vance was brought into the ER in critical condition. According to

doctors it was a very rare illness funeral will be o Saturday the 17th Green-Wood Cen attended by the known for hi

HIS WIFE DIED ON APRIL 15?

BLIP.

TUESDAY APRIL 14 20 15

Professor W.

Ma

PROFESSOR TRAGICA

Thursday, Ap Despite the effo medical staff, a p drama ensued a clinic last night. M was brought tical con

SO, TOMORROW IS THE ANNIVERSARY OF HIS WIFE'S DEATH...

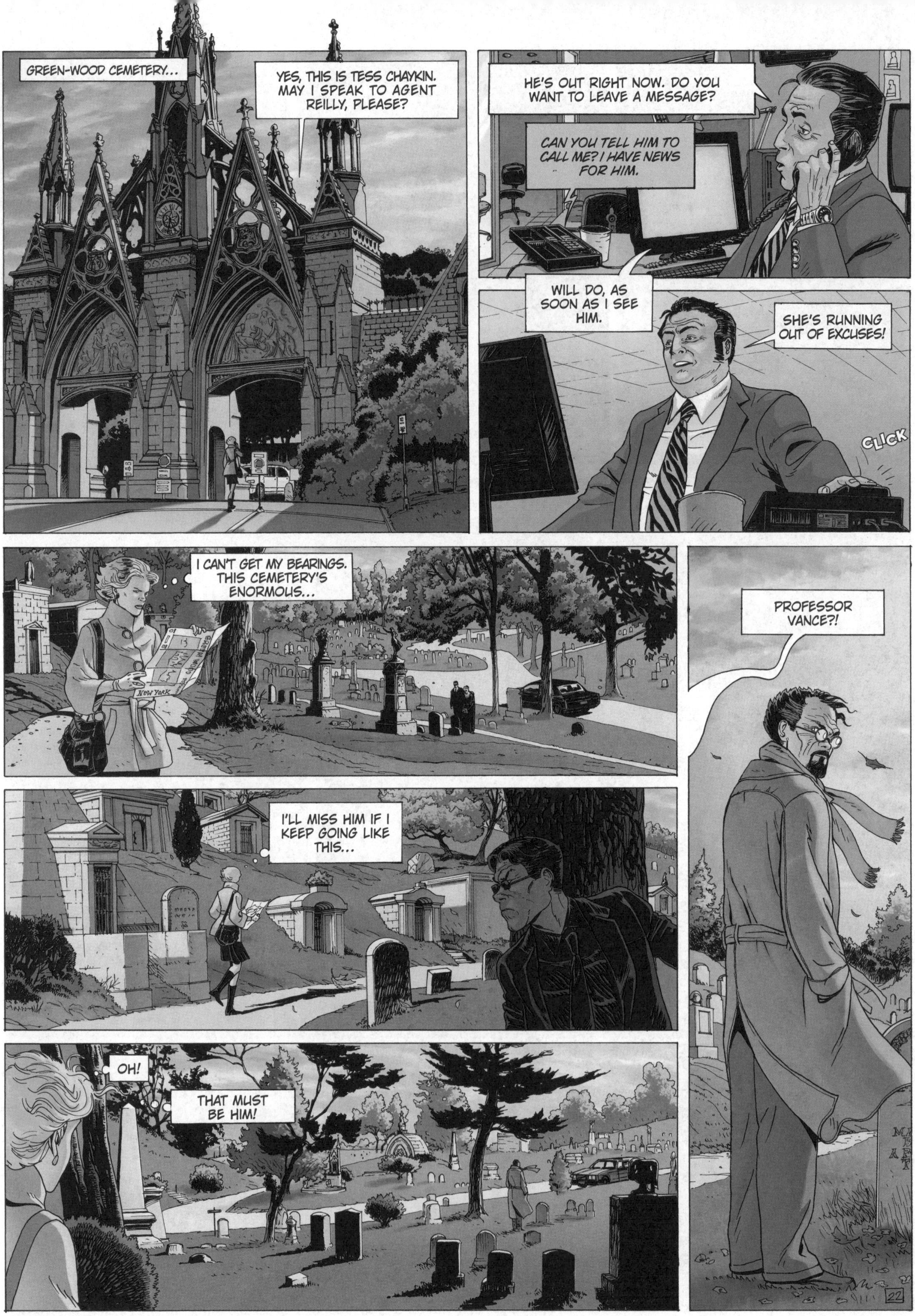
GREEN-WOOD CEMETERY...
YES, THIS IS TESS CHAYKIN. MAY I SPEAK TO AGENT REILLY, PLEASE?
HE'S OUT RIGHT NOW. DO YOU WANT TO LEAVE A MESSAGE?
CAN YOU TELL HIM TO CALL ME? I HAVE NEWS FOR HIM.
WILL DO, AS SOON AS I SEE HIM.
SHE'S RUNNING OUT OF EXCUSES!
CLICK
I CAN'T GET MY BEARINGS. THIS CEMETERY'S ENORMOUS...
NEW YORK
I'LL MISS HIM IF I KEEP GOING LIKE THIS...
OH!
THAT MUST BE HIM!
PROFESSOR VANCE?!
22

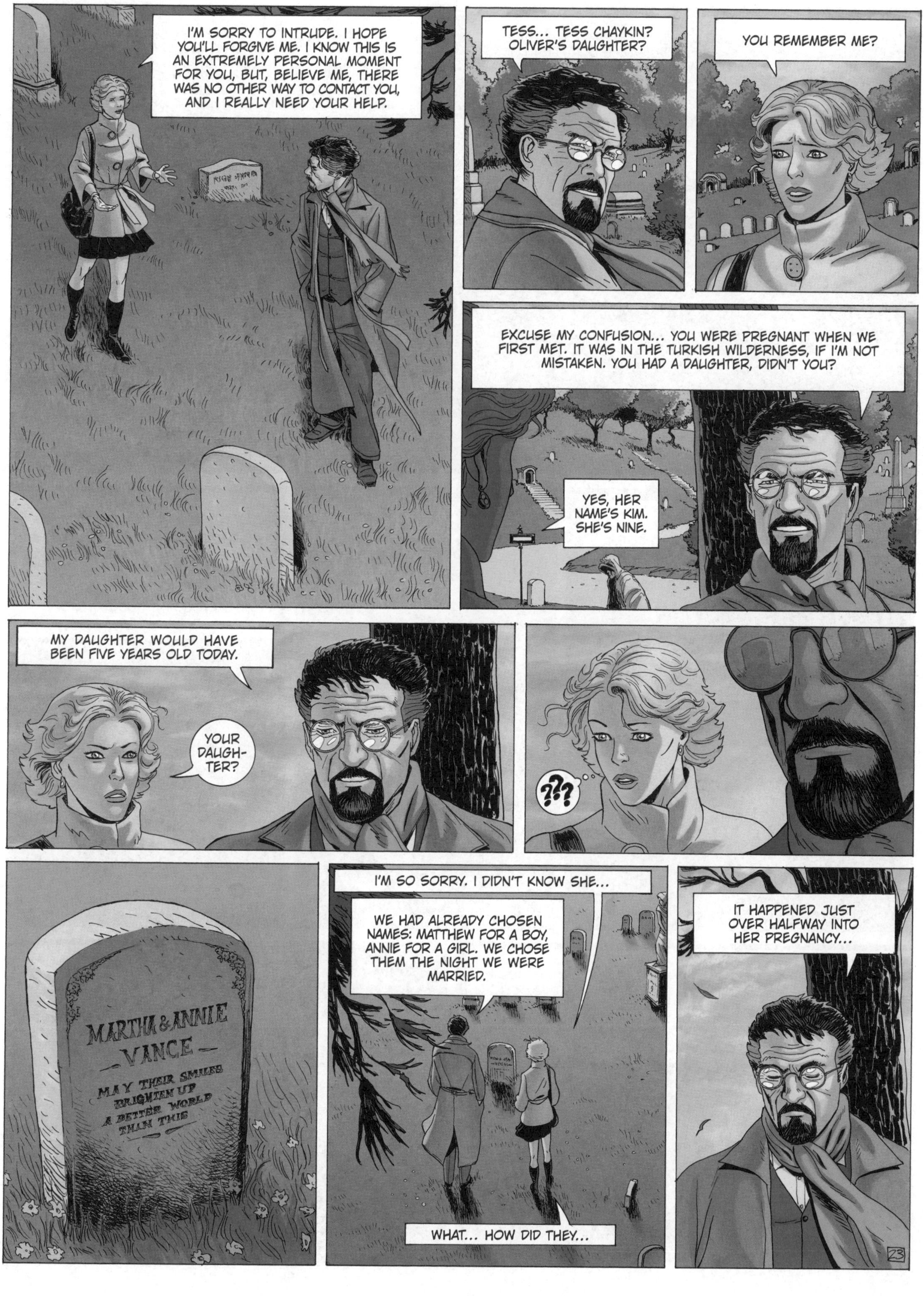

I'M SORRY TO INTRUDE. I HOPE YOU'LL FORGIVE ME. I KNOW THIS IS AN EXTREMELY PERSONAL MOMENT FOR YOU, BUT, BELIEVE ME, THERE WAS NO OTHER WAY TO CONTACT YOU, AND I REALLY NEED YOUR HELP.
TESS... TESS CHAYKIN? OLIVER'S DAUGHTER?
YOU REMEMBER ME?
EXCUSE MY CONFUSION... YOU WERE PREGNANT WHEN WE FIRST MET. IT WAS IN THE TURKISH WILDERNESS, IF I'M NOT MISTAKEN. YOU HAD A DAUGHTER, DIDN'T YOU?
YES, HER NAME'S KIM. SHE'S NINE.
MY DAUGHTER WOULD HAVE BEEN FIVE YEARS OLD TODAY.
YOUR DAUGHTER?
???
MARTHA & ANNIE VANCE
MAY THEIR SMILES BRIGHTEN UP A BETTER WORLD THAN THIS
I'M SO SORRY. I DIDN'T KNOW SHE...
WE HAD ALREADY CHOSEN NAMES: MATTHEW FOR A BOY, ANNIE FOR A GIRL. WE CHOSE THEM THE NIGHT WE WERE MARRIED.
WHAT... HOW DID THEY...
IT HAPPENED JUST OVER HALFWAY INTO HER PREGNANCY...
23

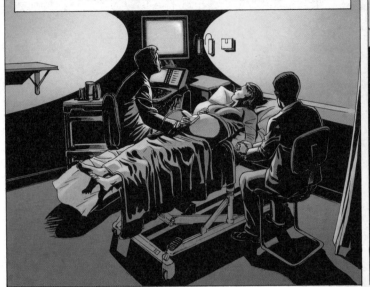

SHE'D BEEN UNDER CLOSE OBSERVATION FROM THE START. IN FACT, WE WERE RATHER OLD TO BE HAVING OUR FIRST CHILD. AND HER FAMILY HAD A HISTORY OF HIGH BLOOD PRESSURE. ANYWAY, SHE DEVELOPED SOMETHING CALLED PRE-ECLAMPSIA. DOCTORS DON'T KNOW WHY IT HAPPENS...

WE WERE TOLD IT WAS PRETTY COMMON, BUT IT CAN BE DEVASTATING, WHICH IT WAS IN MARTHA'S CASE. THERE WAS NOTHING THE DOCTORS COULD DO. THEY TOLD US MARTHA WOULD HAVE TO HAVE AN EMERGENCY ABORTION AND, AS THE FOETUS WAS TOO YOUNG TO HAVE ANY HOPE OF SURVIVING IN AN INCUBATOR...

MARTHA'S CHANCES OF SURVIVAL WERE GETTING SLIMMER BY THE DAY...

WE DIDN'T KNOW WHAT TO DO. WE WERE BELIEVERS, AND AN ABORTION WAS UNTHINK-ABLE TO US. BUT MARTHA'S LIFE WAS AT RISK. SO WE SOUGHT ADVICE FROM OUR SPIRITUAL GUIDE...

...WE ASKED OUR PARISH PRIEST, FATHER MCKAY.

HIS POSITION, THE CHURCH'S POSITION, WAS VERY CLEAR: 'THOU SHALT NOT KILL'. HE SAID IT WOULD BE MURDER, THE MOST HEINOUS OF ALL MURDERS! AN UNSPEAKABLE CRIME... OH, HE WAS VERY ELOQUENT ABOUT IT...

HE SAID WE'D BE KILLING A HUMAN BEING AT THE VERY BEGINNING OF ITS LIFE, THE MOST INNOCENT VICTIM POSSIBLE. A VICTIM WHO DOESN'T UNDERSTAND, A VICTIM WHO CAN'T ARGUE, WHO CAN'T PLEAD FOR ITS LIFE...

HE ASKED US IF WE WOULD DO IT IF WE COULD HEAR ITS CRIES OR SEE ITS TEARS. AND HIS CLOSING ARGUMENT CLINCHED IT: 'IF YOU HAD A ONE-YEAR-OLD BABY, WOULD YOU SACRIFICE IT TO SAVE YOUR OWN LIFE? NO. OF COURSE YOU WOULDN'T. WHAT IF IT WAS ONE MONTH OLD? ONE DAY? WHEN DOES THE CLOCK REALLY START TICKING FOR A LIFE?'

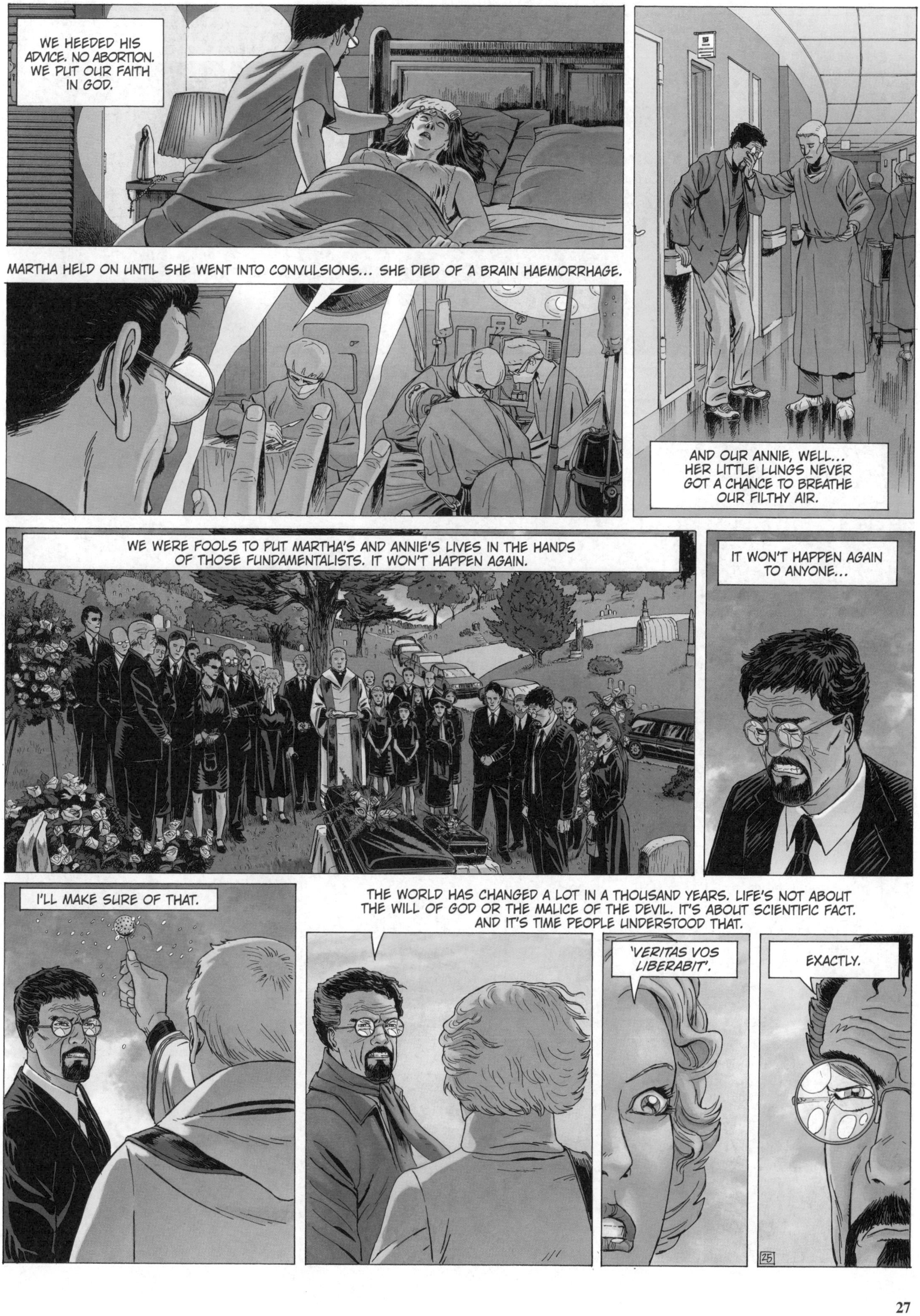
WE HEEDED HIS ADVICE. NO ABORTION. WE PUT OUR FAITH IN GOD.
MARTHA HELD ON UNTIL SHE WENT INTO CONVULSIONS... SHE DIED OF A BRAIN HAEMORRHAGE.
AND OUR ANNIE, WELL... HER LITTLE LUNGS NEVER GOT A CHANCE TO BREATHE OUR FILTHY AIR.
WE WERE FOOLS TO PUT MARTHA'S AND ANNIE'S LIVES IN THE HANDS OF THOSE FUNDAMENTALISTS. IT WON'T HAPPEN AGAIN.
IT WON'T HAPPEN AGAIN TO ANYONE...
I'LL MAKE SURE OF THAT.
THE WORLD HAS CHANGED A LOT IN A THOUSAND YEARS. LIFE'S NOT ABOUT THE WILL OF GOD OR THE MALICE OF THE DEVIL. IT'S ABOUT SCIENTIFIC FACT. AND IT'S TIME PEOPLE UNDERSTOOD THAT.
'VERITAS VOS LIBERABIT'.
EXACTLY.
25

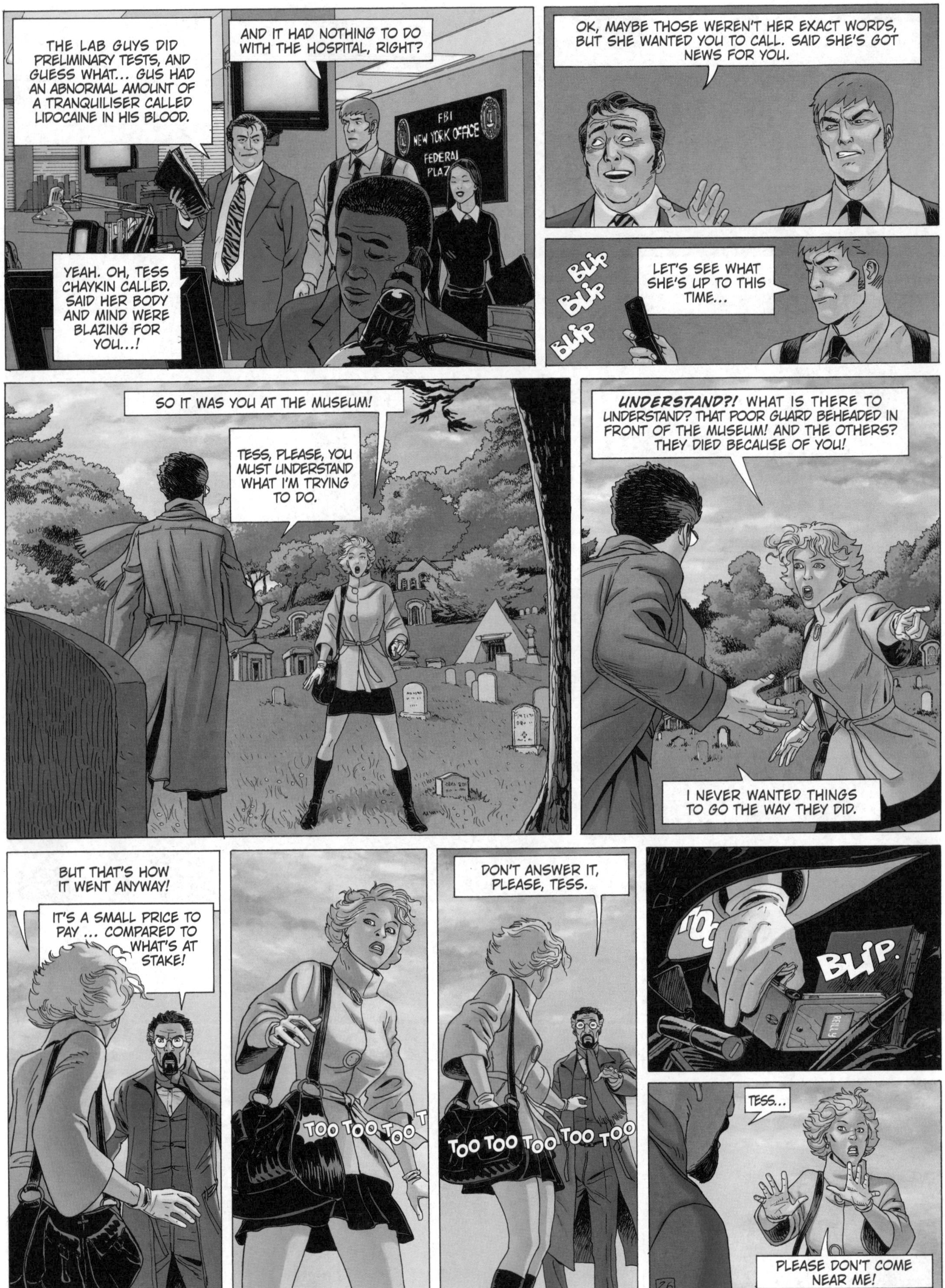
THE LAB GUYS DID PRELIMINARY TESTS, AND GUESS WHAT... GUS HAD AN ABNORMAL AMOUNT OF A TRANQUILISER CALLED LIDOCAINE IN HIS BLOOD.
AND IT HAD NOTHING TO DO WITH THE HOSPITAL, RIGHT?
FBI NEW YORK OFFICE FEDERAL PLAZA
YEAH. OH, TESS CHAYKIN CALLED. SAID HER BODY AND MIND WERE BLAZING FOR YOU...!
OK, MAYBE THOSE WEREN'T HER EXACT WORDS, BUT SHE WANTED YOU TO CALL. SAID SHE'S GOT NEWS FOR YOU.
BLIP BLIP BLIP
LET'S SEE WHAT SHE'S UP TO THIS TIME...
SO IT WAS YOU AT THE MUSEUM!
TESS, PLEASE, YOU MUST UNDERSTAND WHAT I'M TRYING TO DO.
UNDERSTAND?! WHAT IS THERE TO UNDERSTAND? THAT POOR GUARD BEHEADED IN FRONT OF THE MUSEUM! AND THE OTHERS? THEY DIED BECAUSE OF YOU!
I NEVER WANTED THINGS TO GO THE WAY THEY DID.
BUT THAT'S HOW IT WENT ANYWAY!
IT'S A SMALL PRICE TO PAY ... COMPARED TO WHAT'S AT STAKE!
TOO TOO TOO T
DON'T ANSWER IT, PLEASE, TESS.
TOO TOO TOO TOO TOO
BLIP.
REILLY
TESS...
PLEASE DON'T COME NEAR ME!

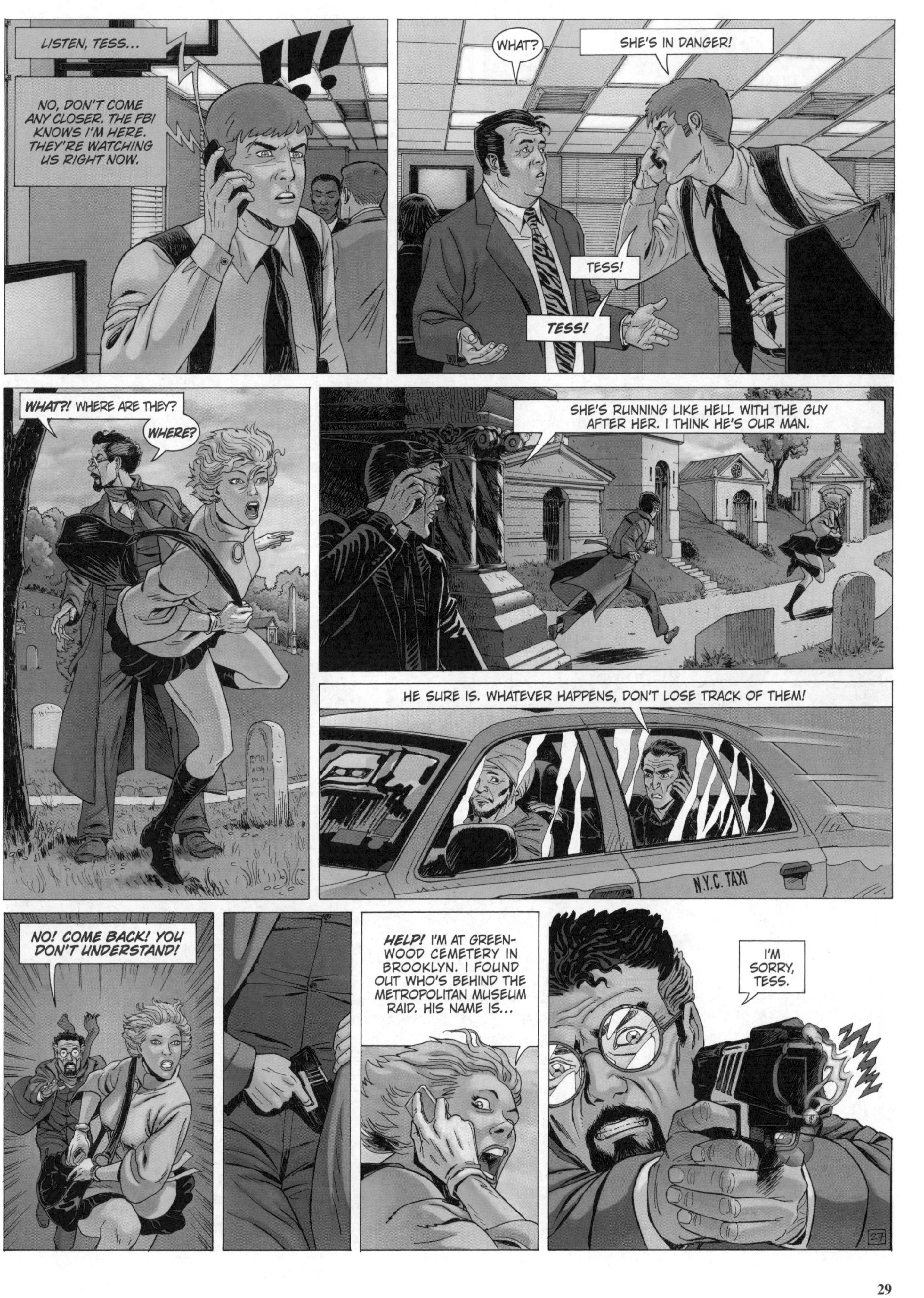

LISTEN, TESS...
NO, DON'T COME ANY CLOSER. THE FBI KNOWS I'M HERE. THEY'RE WATCHING US RIGHT NOW.
!!!
WHAT?
SHE'S IN DANGER!
TESS!
TESS!
WHAT?! WHERE ARE THEY?
WHERE?
SHE'S RUNNING LIKE HELL WITH THE GUY AFTER HER. I THINK HE'S OUR MAN.
HE SURE IS. WHATEVER HAPPENS, DON'T LOSE TRACK OF THEM!
N.Y.C. TAXI
NO! COME BACK! YOU DON'T UNDERSTAND!
HELP! I'M AT GREEN-WOOD CEMETERY IN BROOKLYN. I FOUND OUT WHO'S BEHIND THE METROPOLITAN MUSEUM RAID. HIS NAME IS...
I'M SORRY, TESS.
27

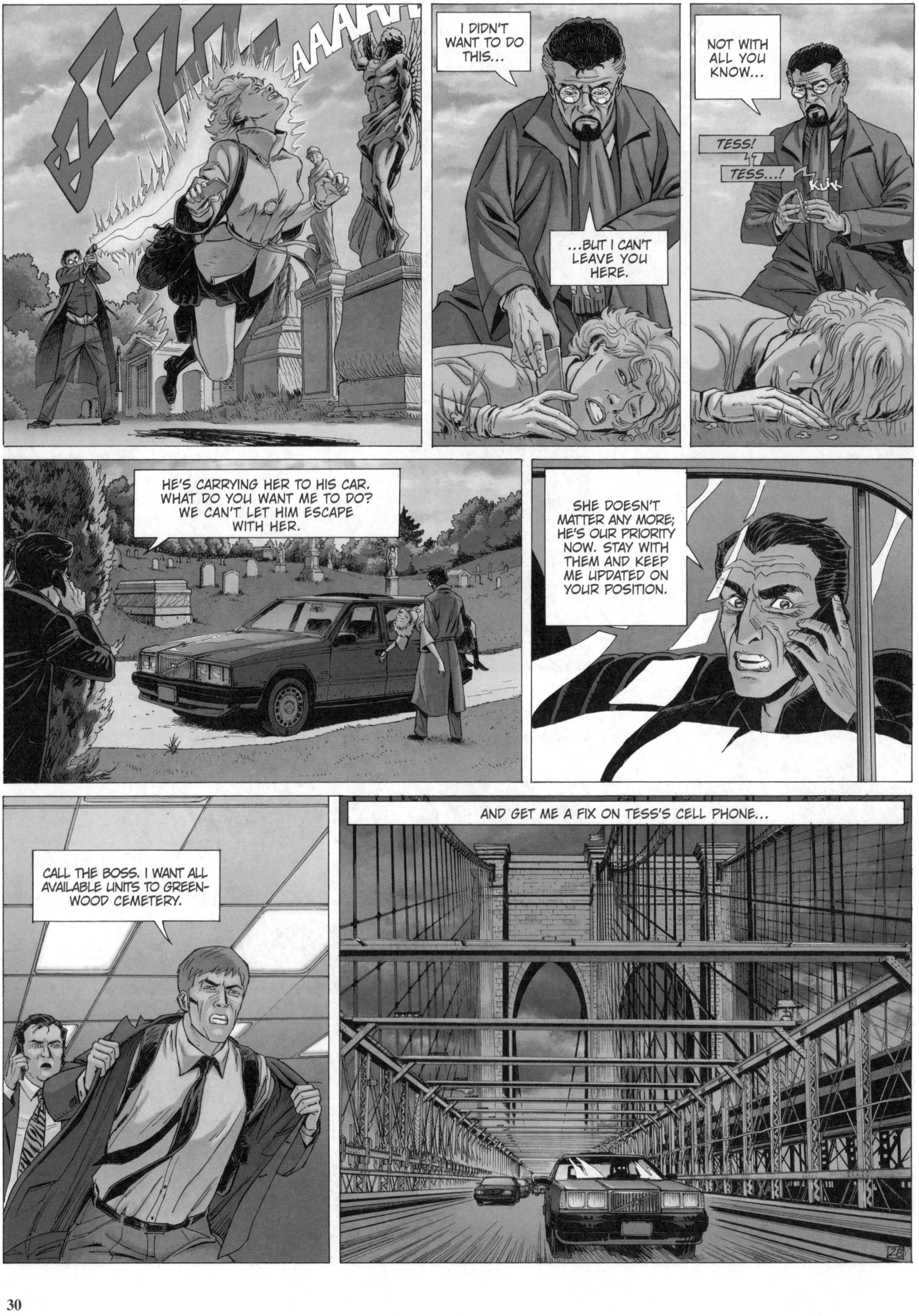
BZZZT
AAAARH
I DIDN'T WANT TO DO THIS...
...BUT I CAN'T LEAVE YOU HERE.
NOT WITH ALL YOU KNOW...
TESS!
TESS...!
KLIK
HE'S CARRYING HER TO HIS CAR. WHAT DO YOU WANT ME TO DO? WE CAN'T LET HIM ESCAPE WITH HER.
SHE DOESN'T MATTER ANY MORE; HE'S OUR PRIORITY NOW. STAY WITH THEM AND KEEP ME UPDATED ON YOUR POSITION.
CALL THE BOSS. I WANT ALL AVAILABLE UNITS TO GREEN-WOOD CEMETERY.
AND GET ME A FIX ON TESS'S CELL PHONE...
28

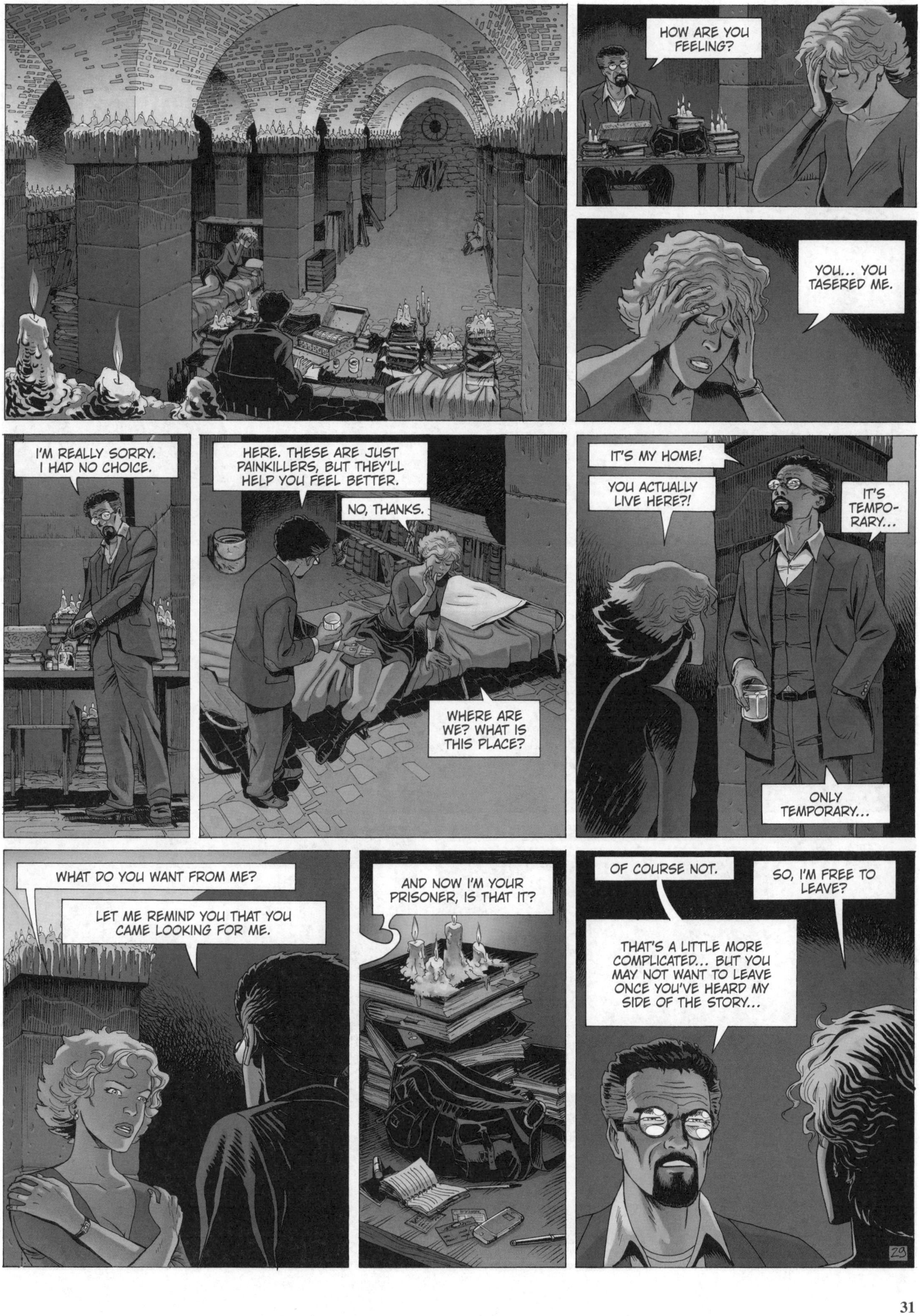
HOW ARE YOU FEELING?
YOU… YOU TASERED ME.
I'M REALLY SORRY. I HAD NO CHOICE.
HERE. THESE ARE JUST PAINKILLERS, BUT THEY'LL HELP YOU FEEL BETTER.
NO, THANKS.
WHERE ARE WE? WHAT IS THIS PLACE?
IT'S MY HOME!
YOU ACTUALLY LIVE HERE?!
IT'S TEMPO-RARY…
ONLY TEMPORARY…
WHAT DO YOU WANT FROM ME?
LET ME REMIND YOU THAT YOU CAME LOOKING FOR ME.
AND NOW I'M YOUR PRISONER, IS THAT IT?
OF COURSE NOT.
SO, I'M FREE TO LEAVE?
THAT'S A LITTLE MORE COMPLICATED… BUT YOU MAY NOT WANT TO LEAVE ONCE YOU'VE HEARD MY SIDE OF THE STORY…
29

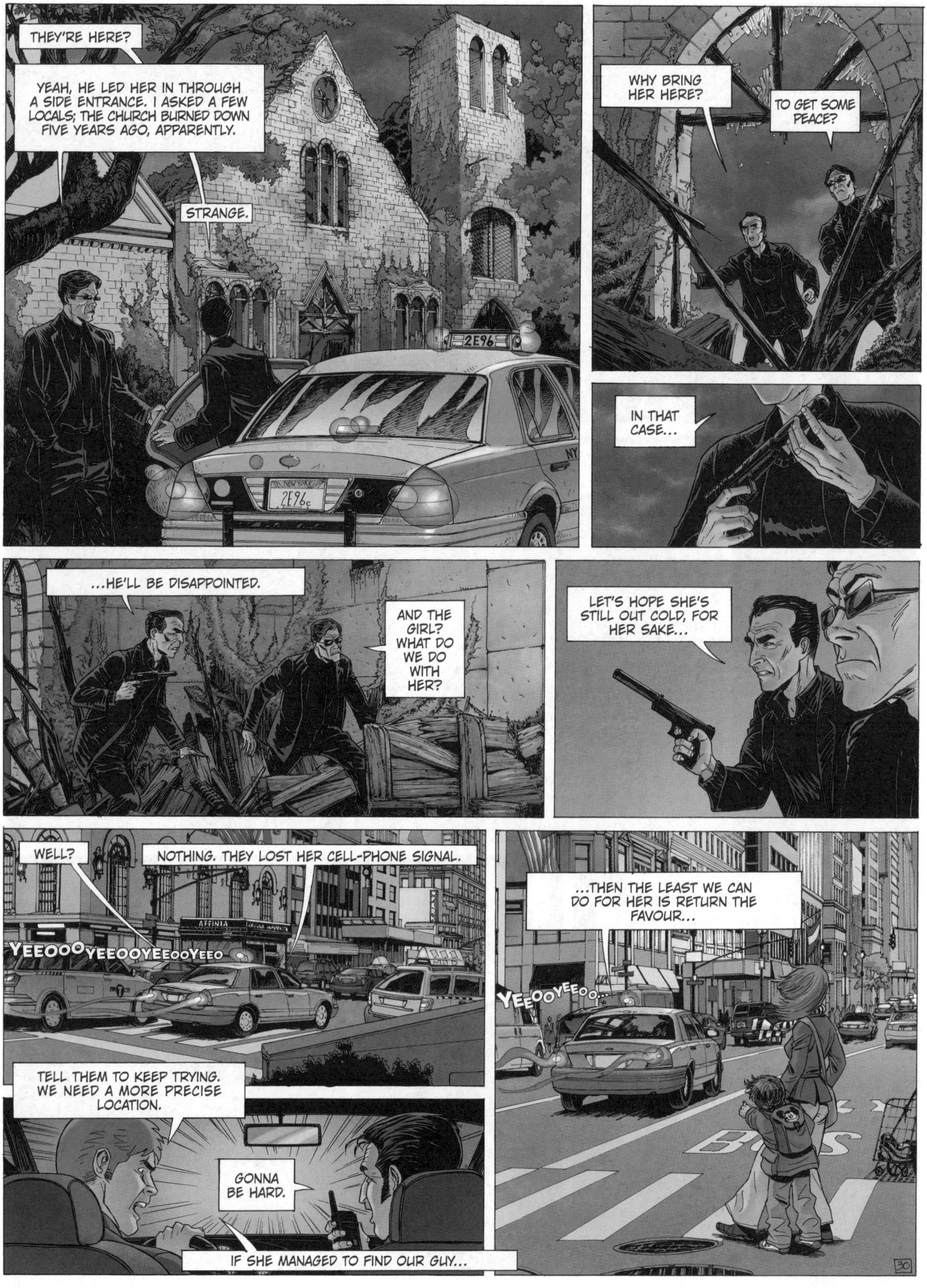

THEY'RE HERE?
YEAH, HE LED HER IN THROUGH A SIDE ENTRANCE. I ASKED A FEW LOCALS; THE CHURCH BURNED DOWN FIVE YEARS AGO, APPARENTLY.
STRANGE.
2E96
NEW YORK
2E96c
NY
WHY BRING HER HERE?
TO GET SOME PEACE?
IN THAT CASE...
...HE'LL BE DISAPPOINTED.
AND THE GIRL? WHAT DO WE DO WITH HER?
LET'S HOPE SHE'S STILL OUT COLD, FOR HER SAKE...
WELL?
NOTHING. THEY LOST HER CELL-PHONE SIGNAL.
AFFINIA
YEEOOOYEEOOYEEooYEEO
TELL THEM TO KEEP TRYING. WE NEED A MORE PRECISE LOCATION.
GONNA BE HARD.
IF SHE MANAGED TO FIND OUR GUY...
...THEN THE LEAST WE CAN DO FOR HER IS RETURN THE FAVOUR...
YEEOOYEEoo...
BUS
30

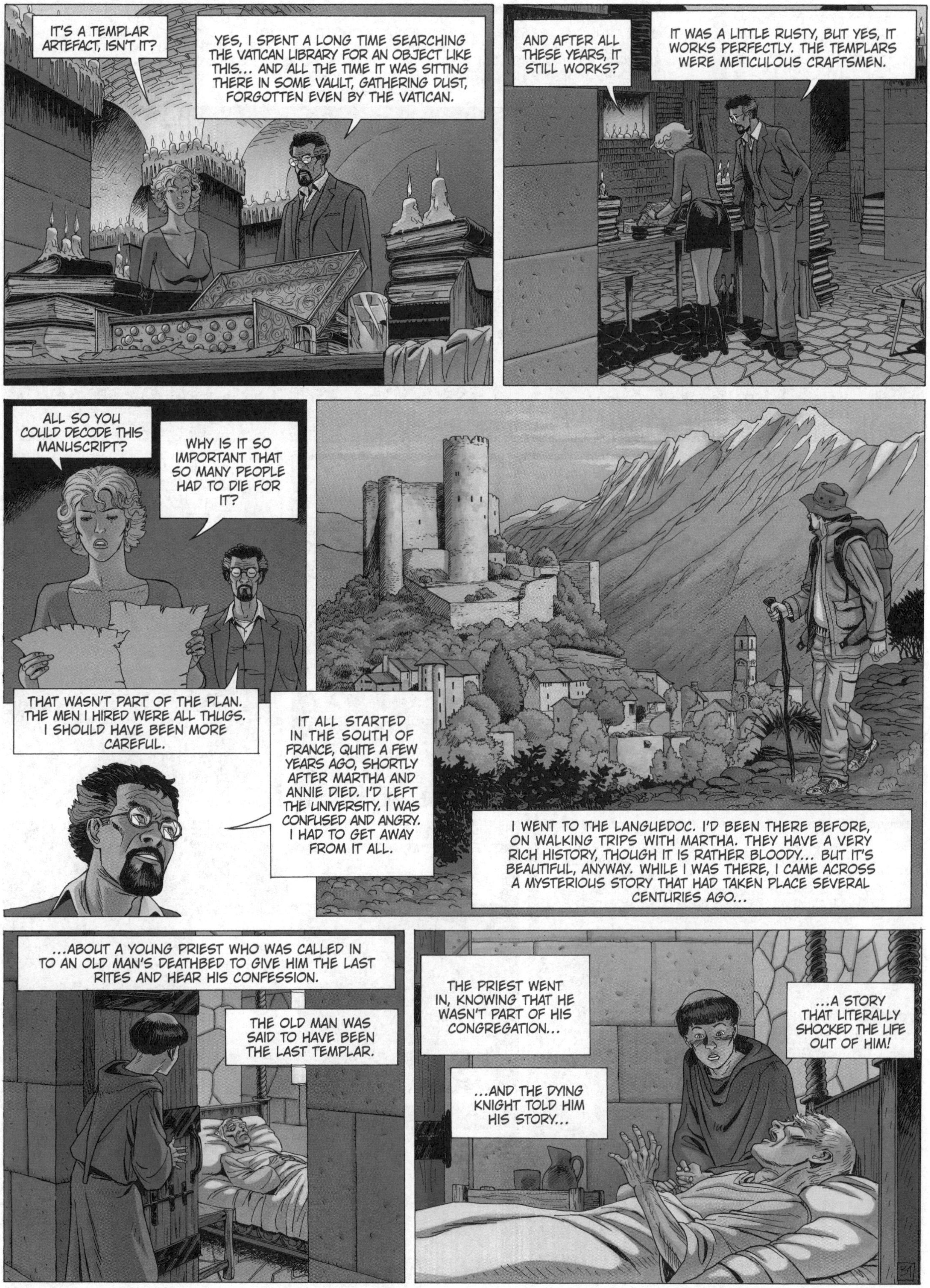
IT'S A TEMPLAR ARTEFACT, ISN'T IT?
YES, I SPENT A LONG TIME SEARCHING THE VATICAN LIBRARY FOR AN OBJECT LIKE THIS... AND ALL THE TIME IT WAS SITTING THERE IN SOME VAULT, GATHERING DUST, FORGOTTEN EVEN BY THE VATICAN.
AND AFTER ALL THESE YEARS, IT STILL WORKS?
IT WAS A LITTLE RUSTY, BUT YES, IT WORKS PERFECTLY. THE TEMPLARS WERE METICULOUS CRAFTSMEN.
ALL SO YOU COULD DECODE THIS MANUSCRIPT?
WHY IS IT SO IMPORTANT THAT SO MANY PEOPLE HAD TO DIE FOR IT?
THAT WASN'T PART OF THE PLAN. THE MEN I HIRED WERE ALL THUGS. I SHOULD HAVE BEEN MORE CAREFUL.
IT ALL STARTED IN THE SOUTH OF FRANCE, QUITE A FEW YEARS AGO, SHORTLY AFTER MARTHA AND ANNIE DIED. I'D LEFT THE UNIVERSITY. I WAS CONFUSED AND ANGRY. I HAD TO GET AWAY FROM IT ALL.
I WENT TO THE LANGUEDOC. I'D BEEN THERE BEFORE, ON WALKING TRIPS WITH MARTHA. THEY HAVE A VERY RICH HISTORY, THOUGH IT IS RATHER BLOODY... BUT IT'S BEAUTIFUL, ANYWAY. WHILE I WAS THERE, I CAME ACROSS A MYSTERIOUS STORY THAT HAD TAKEN PLACE SEVERAL CENTURIES AGO...
...ABOUT A YOUNG PRIEST WHO WAS CALLED IN TO AN OLD MAN'S DEATHBED TO GIVE HIM THE LAST RITES AND HEAR HIS CONFESSION.
THE OLD MAN WAS SAID TO HAVE BEEN THE LAST TEMPLAR.
THE PRIEST WENT IN, KNOWING THAT HE WASN'T PART OF HIS CONGREGATION...
...AND THE DYING KNIGHT TOLD HIM HIS STORY...
...A STORY THAT LITERALLY SHOCKED THE LIFE OUT OF HIM!
31

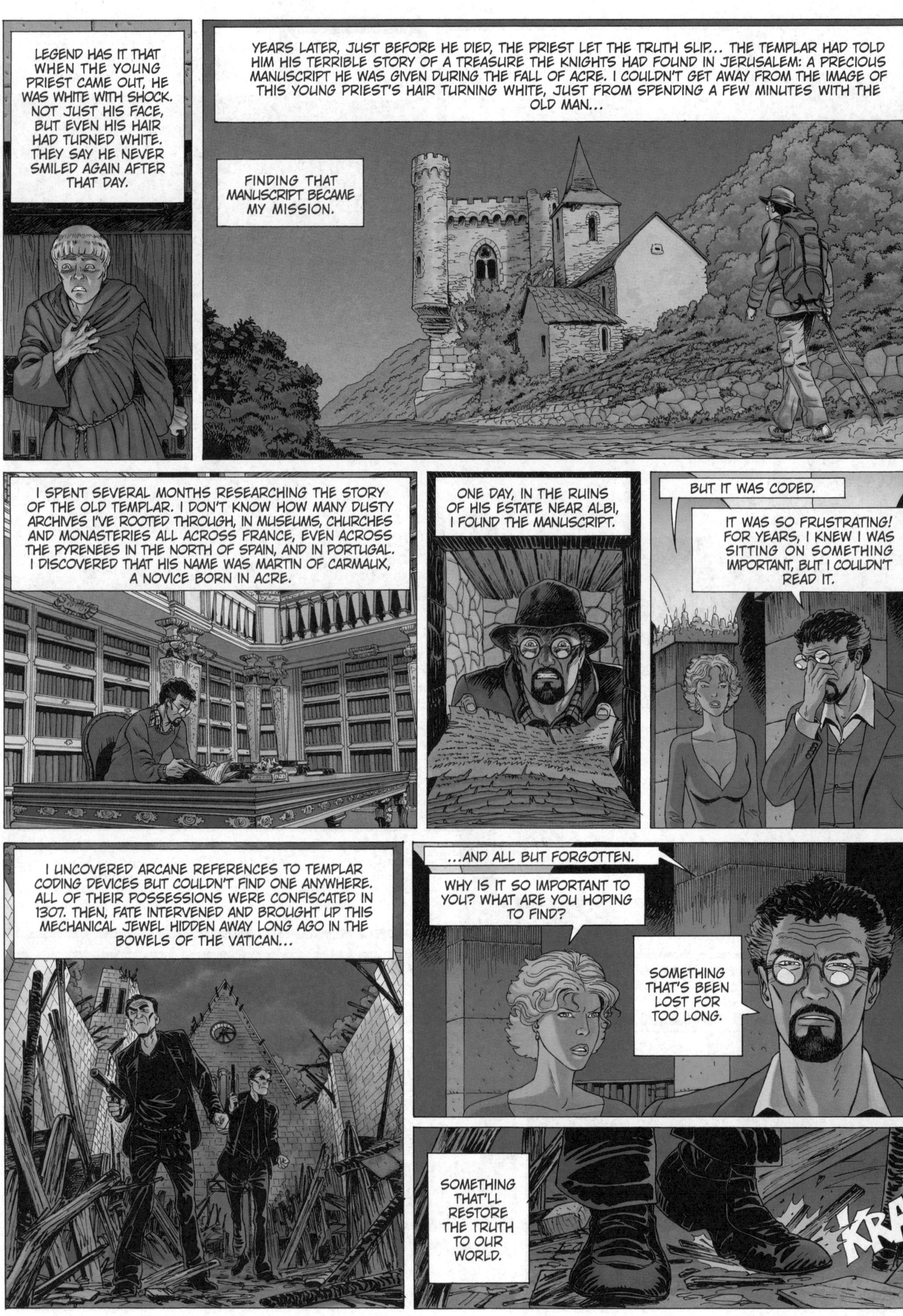
LEGEND HAS IT THAT WHEN THE YOUNG PRIEST CAME OUT, HE WAS WHITE WITH SHOCK. NOT JUST HIS FACE, BUT EVEN HIS HAIR HAD TURNED WHITE. THEY SAY HE NEVER SMILED AGAIN AFTER THAT DAY.
YEARS LATER, JUST BEFORE HE DIED, THE PRIEST LET THE TRUTH SLIP... THE TEMPLAR HAD TOLD HIM HIS TERRIBLE STORY OF A TREASURE THE KNIGHTS HAD FOUND IN JERUSALEM: A PRECIOUS MANUSCRIPT HE WAS GIVEN DURING THE FALL OF ACRE. I COULDN'T GET AWAY FROM THE IMAGE OF THIS YOUNG PRIEST'S HAIR TURNING WHITE, JUST FROM SPENDING A FEW MINUTES WITH THE OLD MAN...
FINDING THAT MANUSCRIPT BECAME MY MISSION.
I SPENT SEVERAL MONTHS RESEARCHING THE STORY OF THE OLD TEMPLAR. I DON'T KNOW HOW MANY DUSTY ARCHIVES I'VE ROOTED THROUGH, IN MUSEUMS, CHURCHES AND MONASTERIES ALL ACROSS FRANCE, EVEN ACROSS THE PYRENEES IN THE NORTH OF SPAIN, AND IN PORTUGAL. I DISCOVERED THAT HIS NAME WAS MARTIN OF CARMAUX, A NOVICE BORN IN ACRE.
ONE DAY, IN THE RUINS OF HIS ESTATE NEAR ALBI, I FOUND THE MANUSCRIPT.
BUT IT WAS CODED.
IT WAS SO FRUSTRATING! FOR YEARS, I KNEW I WAS SITTING ON SOMETHING IMPORTANT, BUT I COULDN'T READ IT.
I UNCOVERED ARCANE REFERENCES TO TEMPLAR CODING DEVICES BUT COULDN'T FIND ONE ANYWHERE. ALL OF THEIR POSSESSIONS WERE CONFISCATED IN 1307. THEN, FATE INTERVENED AND BROUGHT UP THIS MECHANICAL JEWEL HIDDEN AWAY LONG AGO IN THE BOWELS OF THE VATICAN...
...AND ALL BUT FORGOTTEN.
WHY IS IT SO IMPORTANT TO YOU? WHAT ARE YOU HOPING TO FIND?
SOMETHING THAT'S BEEN LOST FOR TOO LONG.
SOMETHING THAT'LL RESTORE THE TRUTH TO OUR WORLD.
KRAK!
32

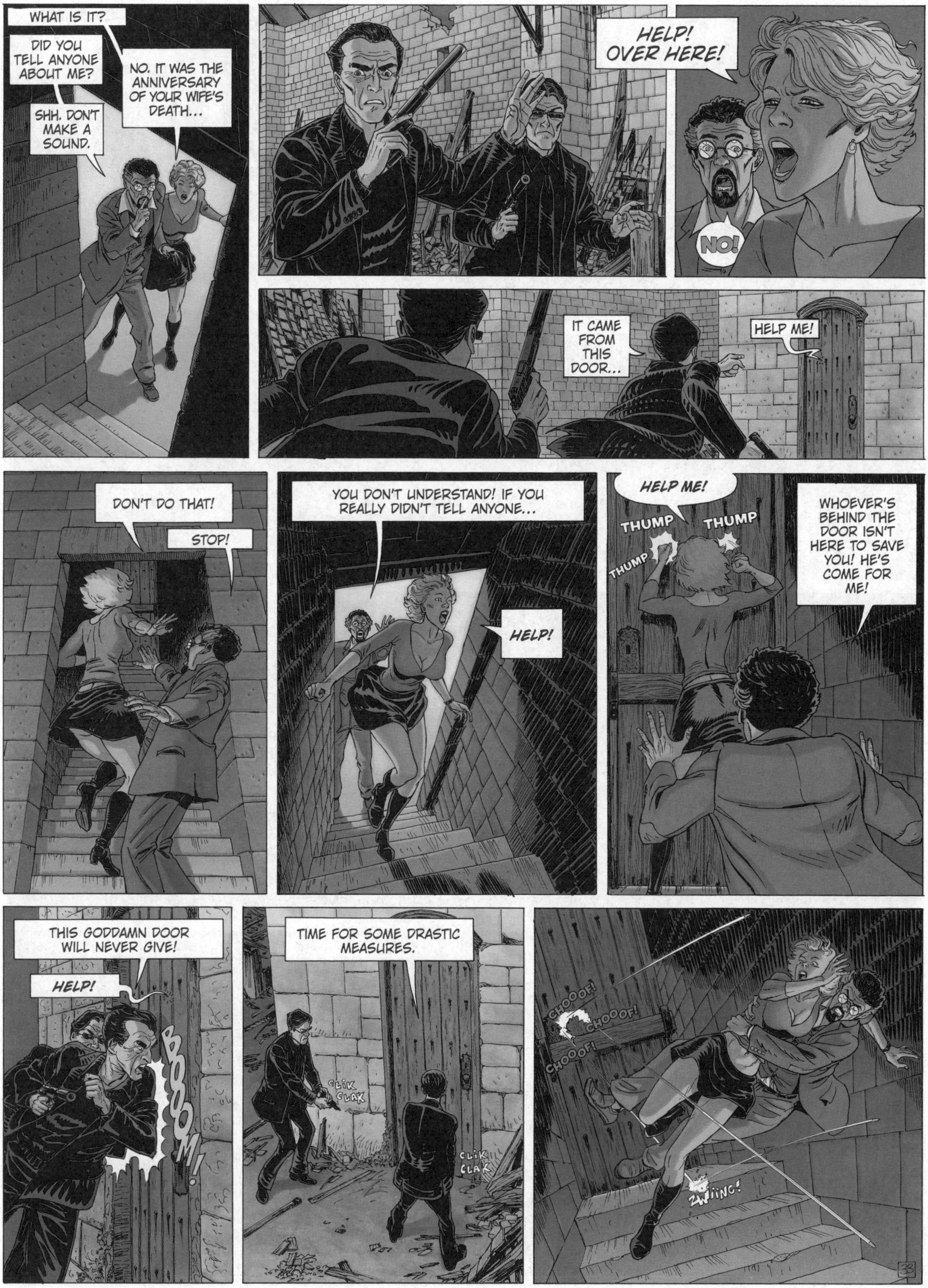

WHAT IS IT?
DID YOU TELL ANYONE ABOUT ME?
NO. IT WAS THE ANNIVERSARY OF YOUR WIFE'S DEATH...
SHH. DON'T MAKE A SOUND.
HELP! OVER HERE!
NO!
IT CAME FROM THIS DOOR...
HELP ME!
DON'T DO THAT!
STOP!
YOU DON'T UNDERSTAND! IF YOU REALLY DIDN'T TELL ANYONE...
HELP!
HELP ME!
THUMP
THUMP
THUMP
WHOEVER'S BEHIND THE DOOR ISN'T HERE TO SAVE YOU! HE'S COME FOR ME!
THIS GODDAMN DOOR WILL NEVER GIVE!
HELP!
BOOOOM!
TIME FOR SOME DRASTIC MEASURES.
CLIK CLAK
CLIK CLAK
CHOOOF!
CHOOOF!
CHOOOF!
ZWIING!
33

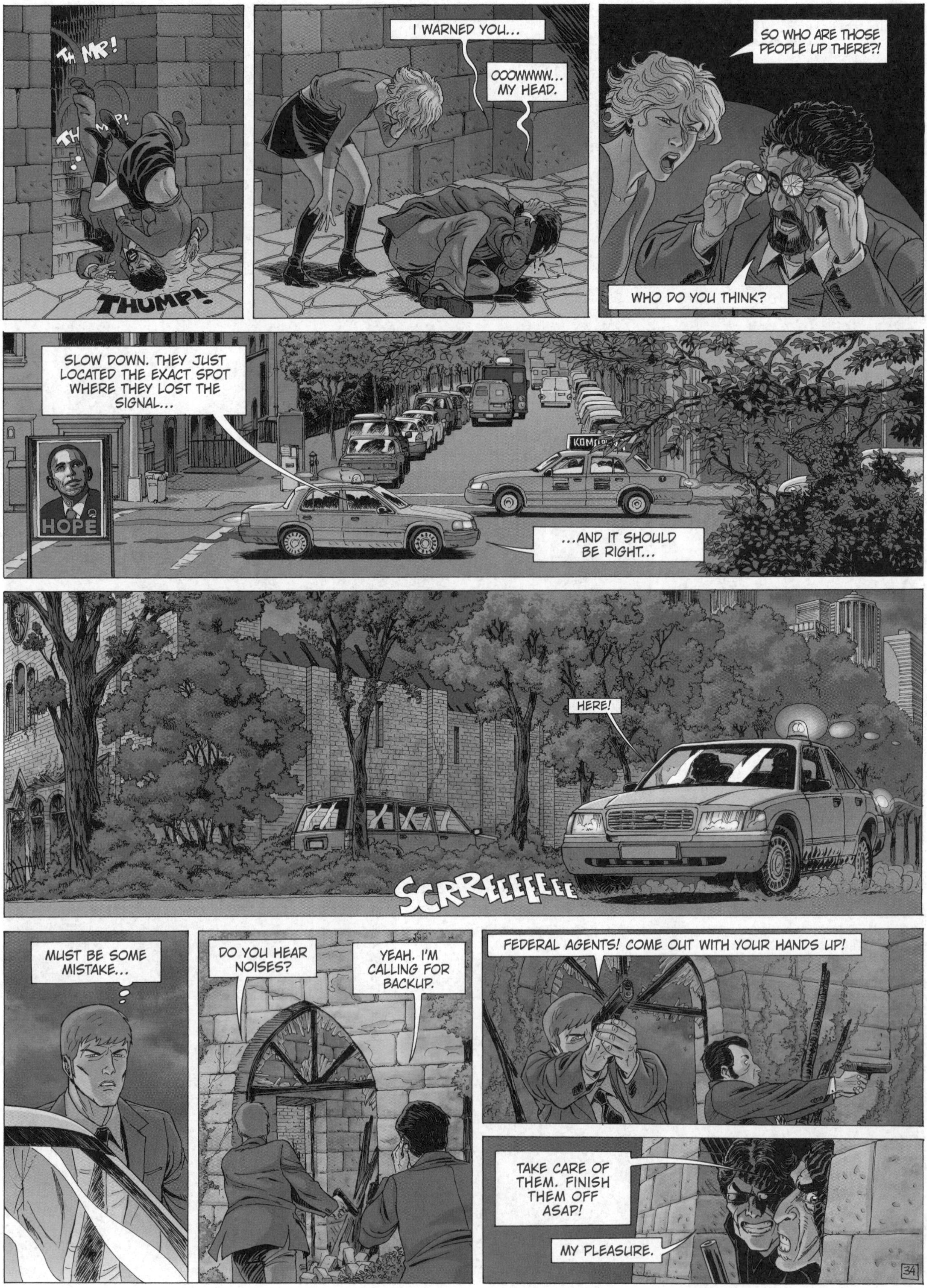
THUMP!
THUMP!
THUMP!
I WARNED YOU...
OOOWWWW... MY HEAD.
SO WHO ARE THOSE PEOPLE UP THERE?!
WHO DO YOU THINK?
SLOW DOWN. THEY JUST LOCATED THE EXACT SPOT WHERE THEY LOST THE SIGNAL...
HOPE
...AND IT SHOULD BE RIGHT...
HERE!
SCRREEEEEEE
MUST BE SOME MISTAKE...
DO YOU HEAR NOISES?
YEAH. I'M CALLING FOR BACKUP.
FEDERAL AGENTS! COME OUT WITH YOUR HANDS UP!
TAKE CARE OF THEM. FINISH THEM OFF ASAP!
MY PLEASURE.
34

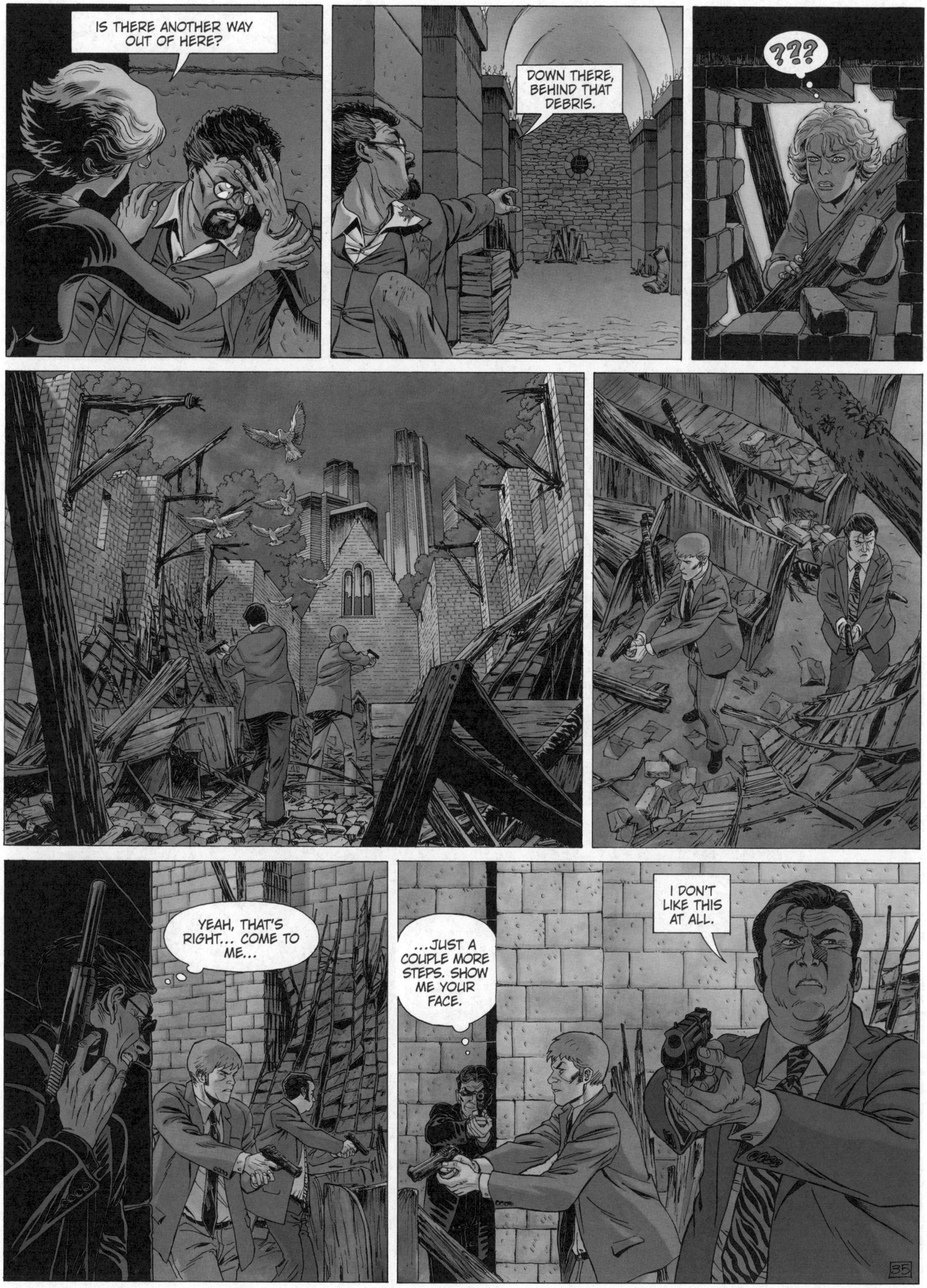

IS THERE ANOTHER WAY OUT OF HERE?
DOWN THERE, BEHIND THAT DEBRIS.
???
YEAH, THAT'S RIGHT... COME TO ME...
...JUST A COUPLE MORE STEPS. SHOW ME YOUR FACE.
I DON'T LIKE THIS AT ALL.
35

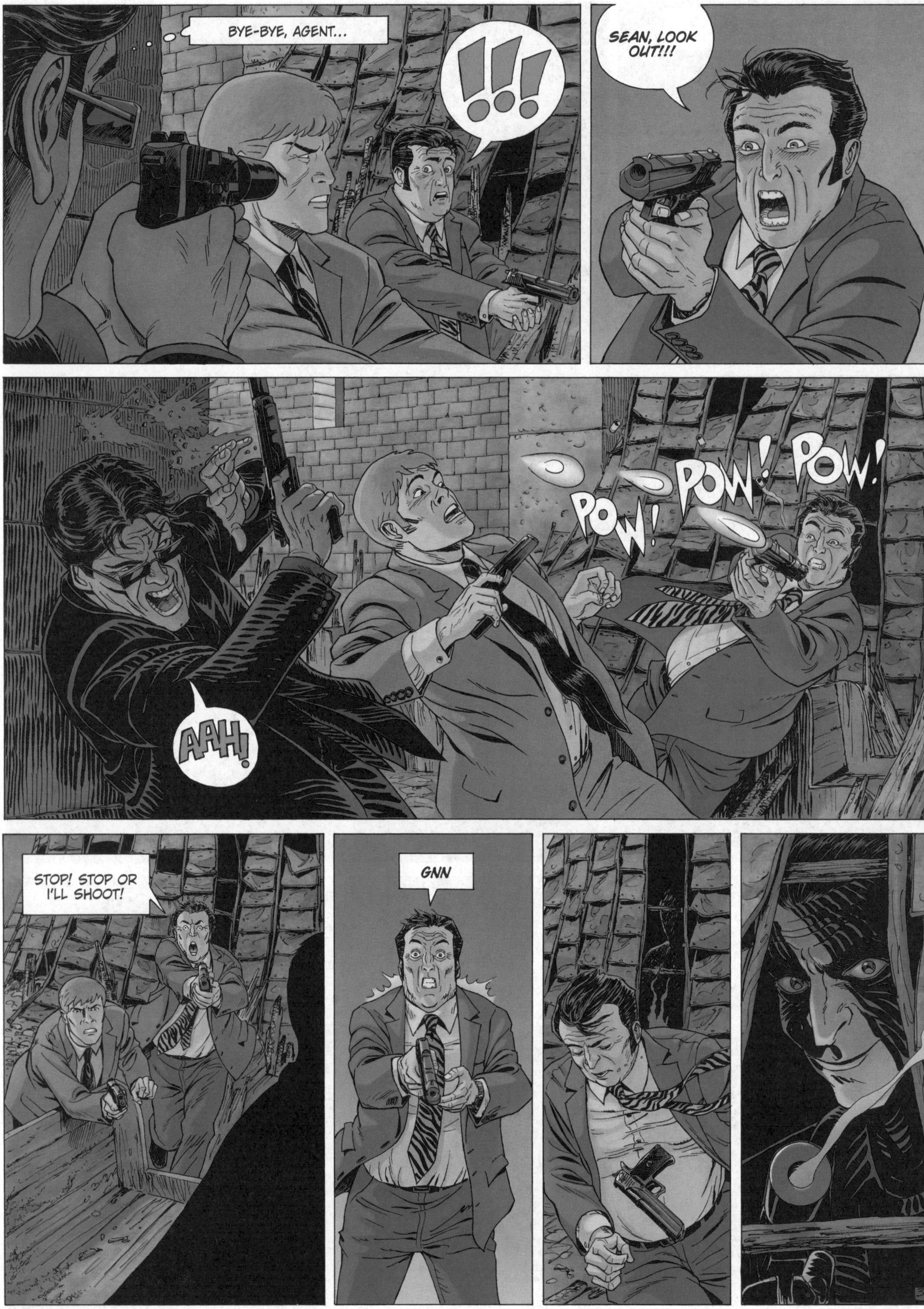
BYE-BYE, AGENT...
!!!
SEAN, LOOK OUT!!!
POW! POW! POW!
AAH!
STOP! STOP OR I'LL SHOOT!
GNN

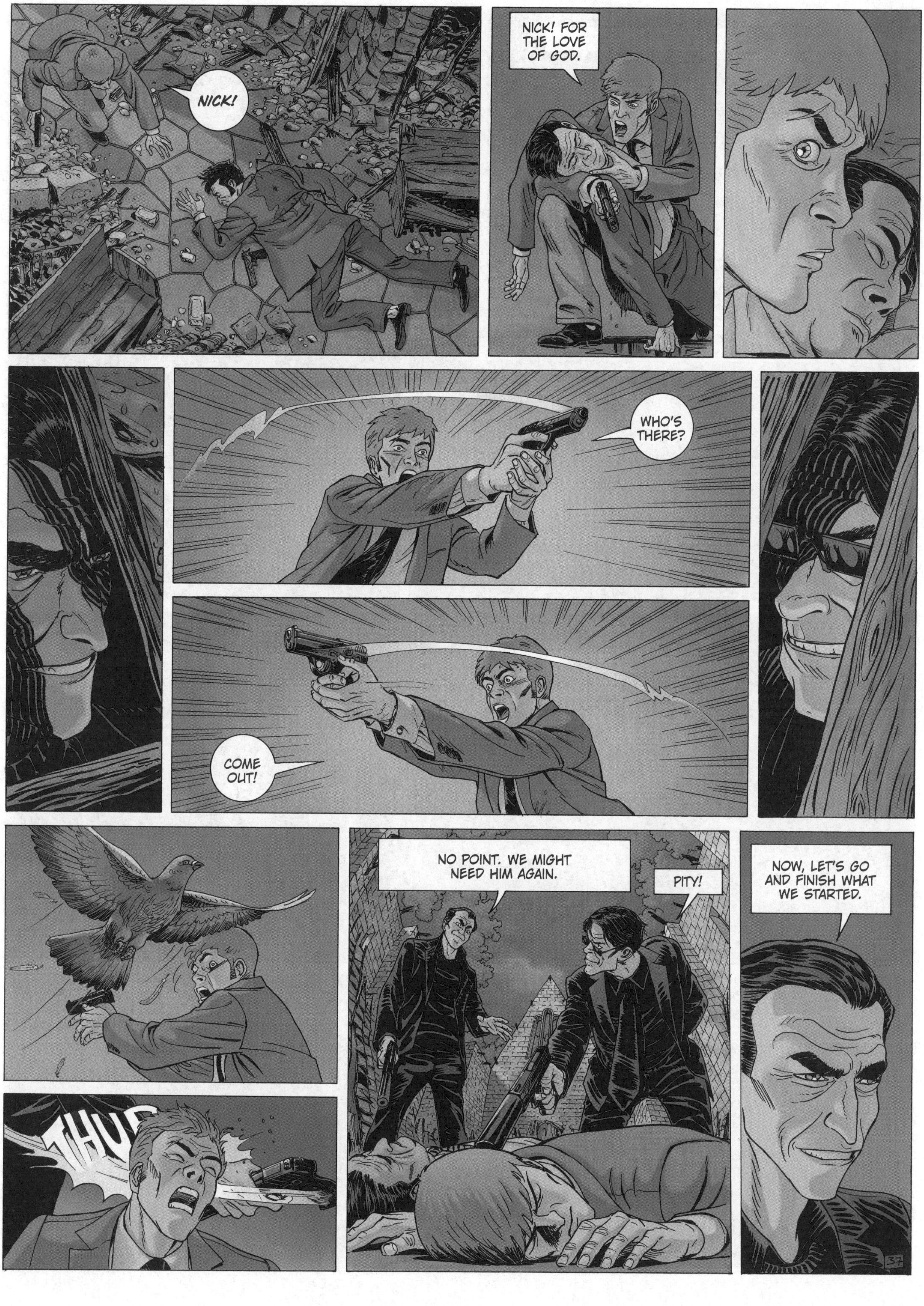
NICK!
NICK! FOR THE LOVE OF GOD.
WHO'S THERE?
COME OUT!
THUD
NO POINT. WE MIGHT NEED HIM AGAIN.
PITY!
NOW, LET'S GO AND FINISH WHAT WE STARTED.
37

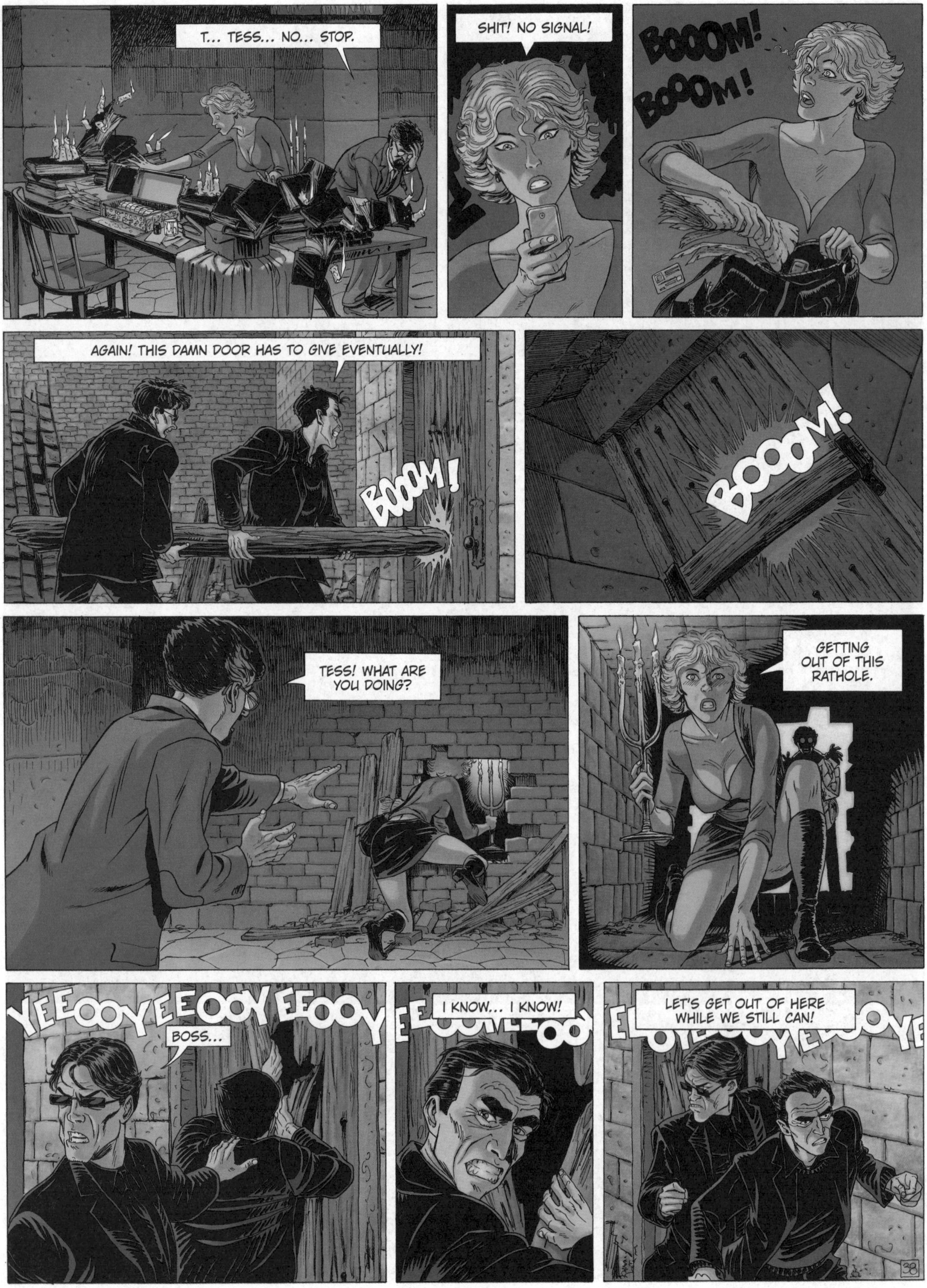

T... TESS... NO... STOP.
SHIT! NO SIGNAL!
BOOOM!
BOOOM!
AGAIN! THIS DAMN DOOR HAS TO GIVE EVENTUALLY!
BOOOM!
BOOOM!
TESS! WHAT ARE YOU DOING?
GETTING OUT OF THIS RATHOLE.
YEEOOYEEOOYEEOOY
BOSS...
I KNOW... I KNOW!
LET'S GET OUT OF HERE WHILE WE STILL CAN!
38

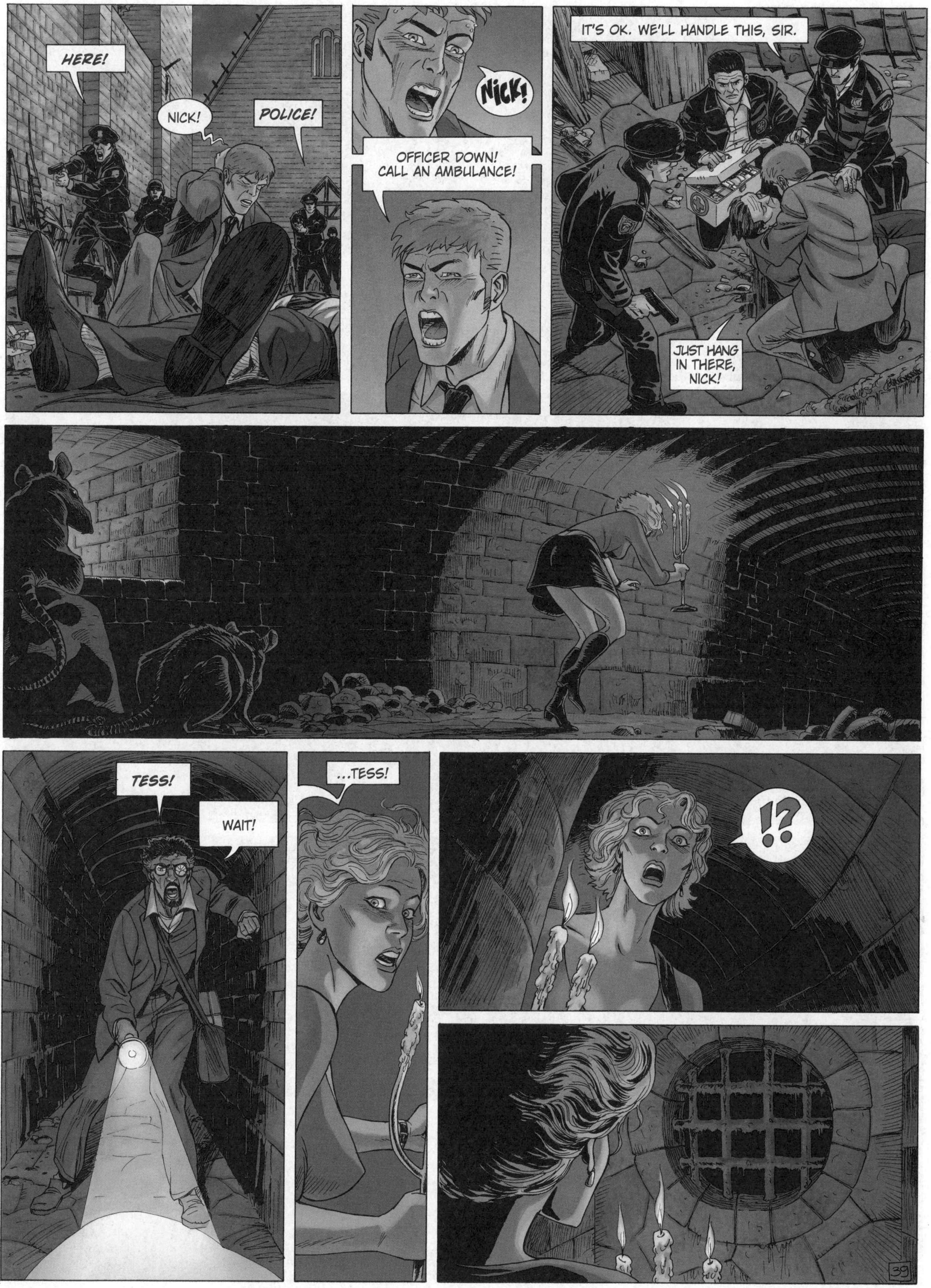
HERE!
NICK!
POLICE!
NICK!
OFFICER DOWN! CALL AN AMBULANCE!
IT'S OK. WE'LL HANDLE THIS, SIR.
JUST HANG IN THERE, NICK!
TESS!
WAIT!
...TESS!
!?
39

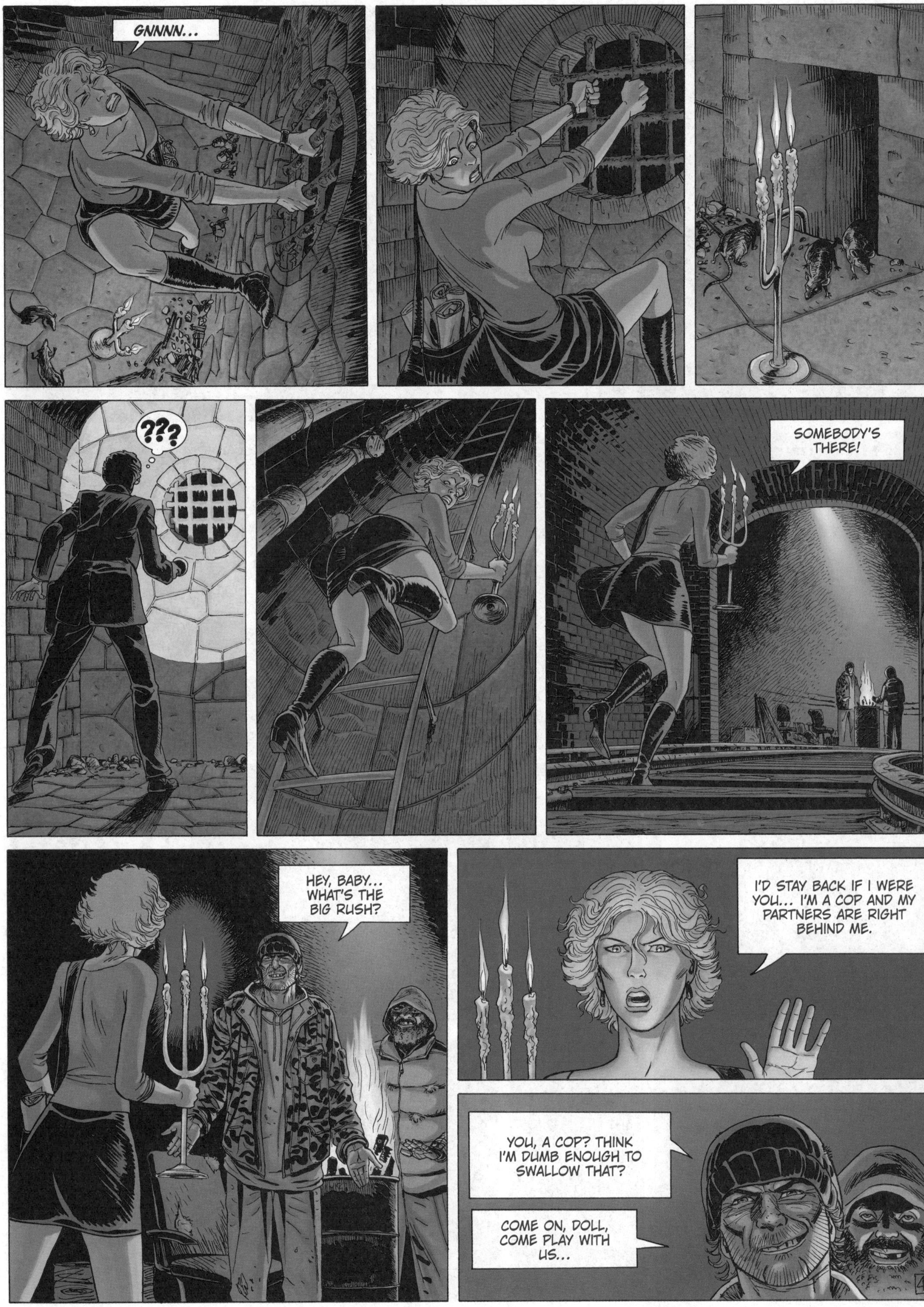

GNNNN...
???
SOMEBODY'S THERE!
HEY, BABY... WHAT'S THE BIG RUSH?
I'D STAY BACK IF I WERE YOU... I'M A COP AND MY PARTNERS ARE RIGHT BEHIND ME.
YOU, A COP? THINK I'M DUMB ENOUGH TO SWALLOW THAT?
COME ON, DOLL, COME PLAY WITH US...

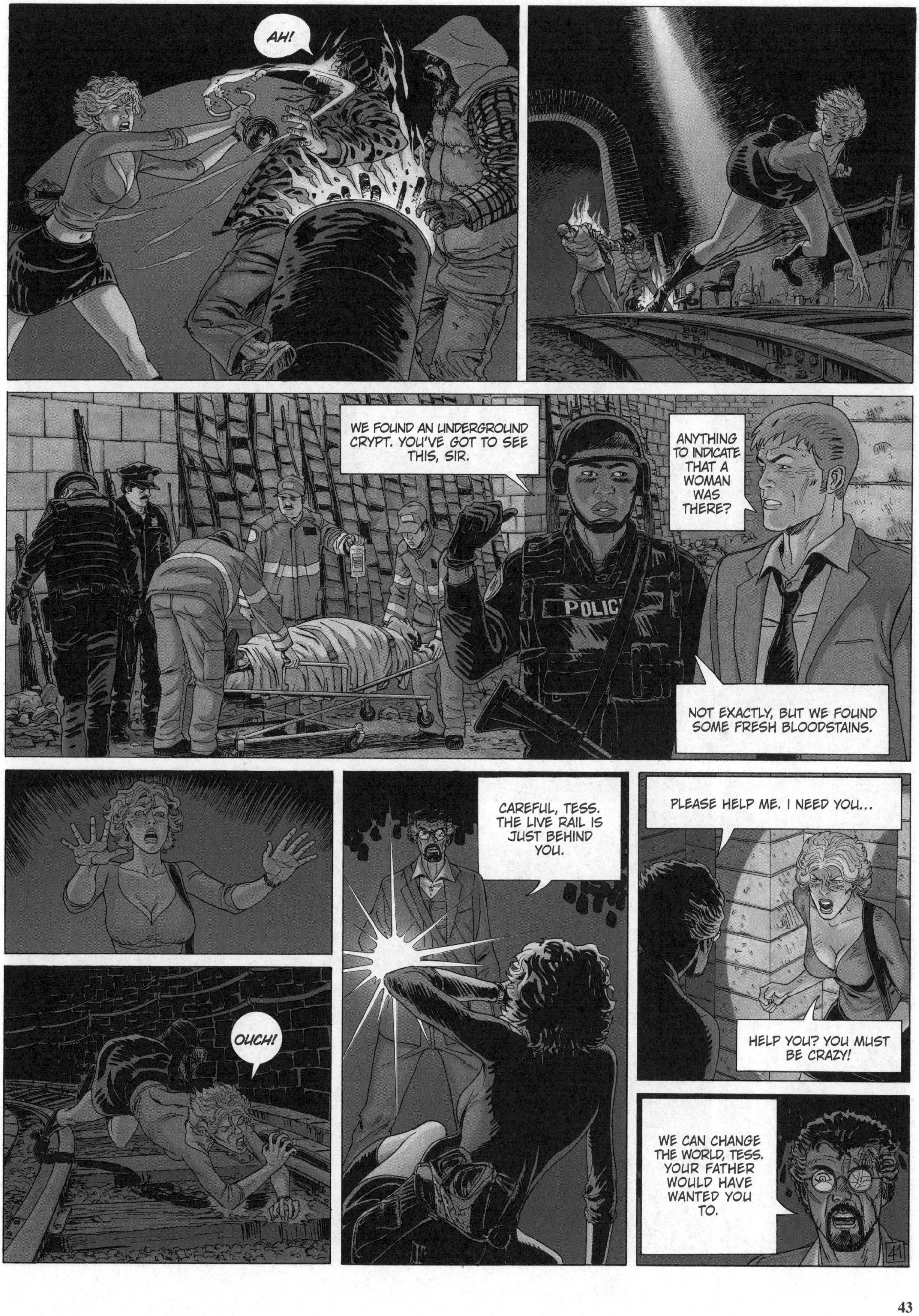
AH!
WE FOUND AN UNDERGROUND CRYPT. YOU'VE GOT TO SEE THIS, SIR.
ANYTHING TO INDICATE THAT A WOMAN WAS THERE?
NOT EXACTLY, BUT WE FOUND SOME FRESH BLOODSTAINS.
CAREFUL, TESS. THE LIVE RAIL IS JUST BEHIND YOU.
OUCH!
PLEASE HELP ME. I NEED YOU...
HELP YOU? YOU MUST BE CRAZY!
WE CAN CHANGE THE WORLD, TESS. YOUR FATHER WOULD HAVE WANTED YOU TO.
41

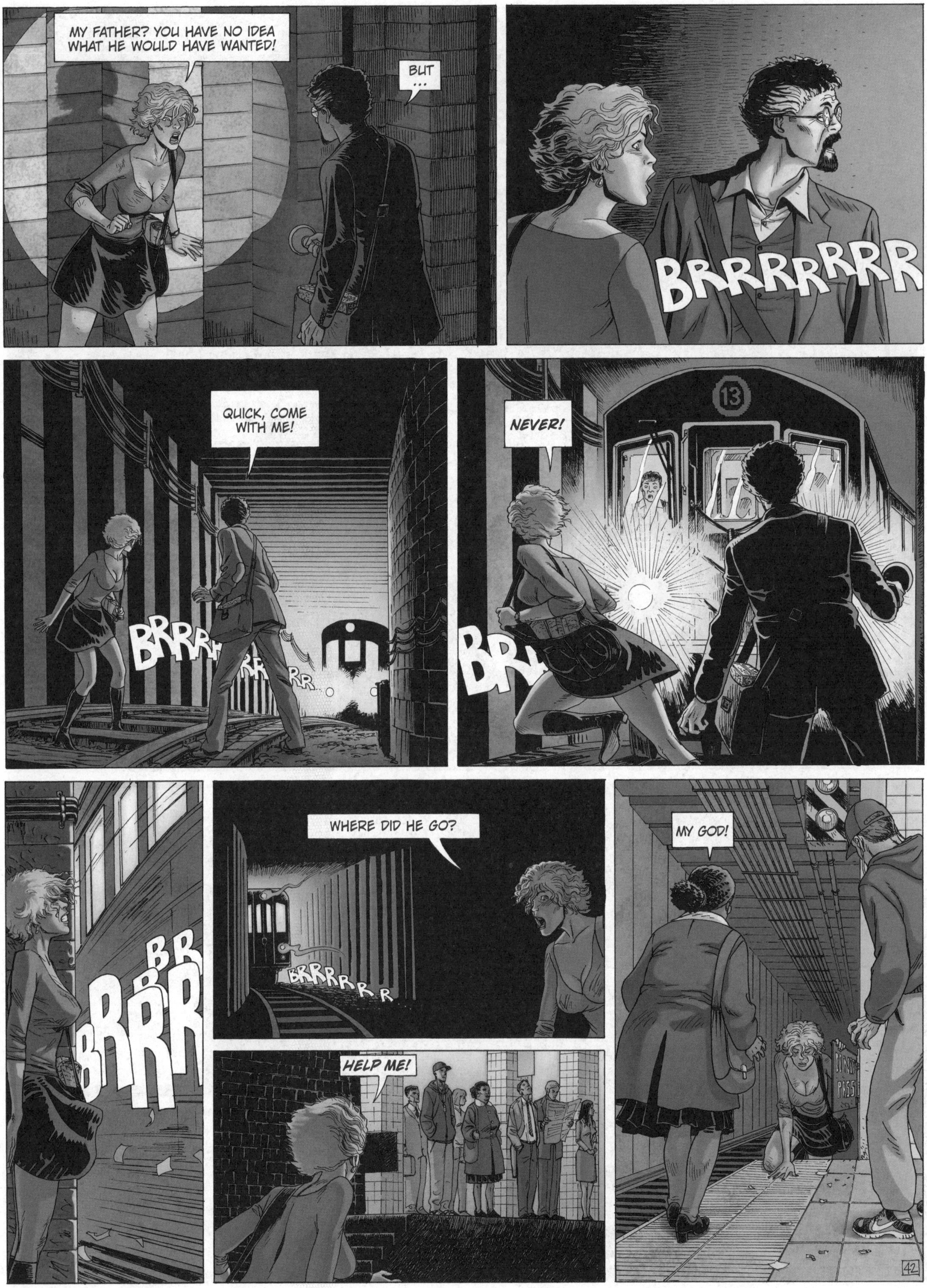
MY FATHER? YOU HAVE NO IDEA WHAT HE WOULD HAVE WANTED!
BUT ...
BRRRRRRRR
QUICK, COME WITH ME!
BRRRRRRR
NEVER!
WHERE DID HE GO?
BRRRRRRR
HELP ME!
MY GOD!
42

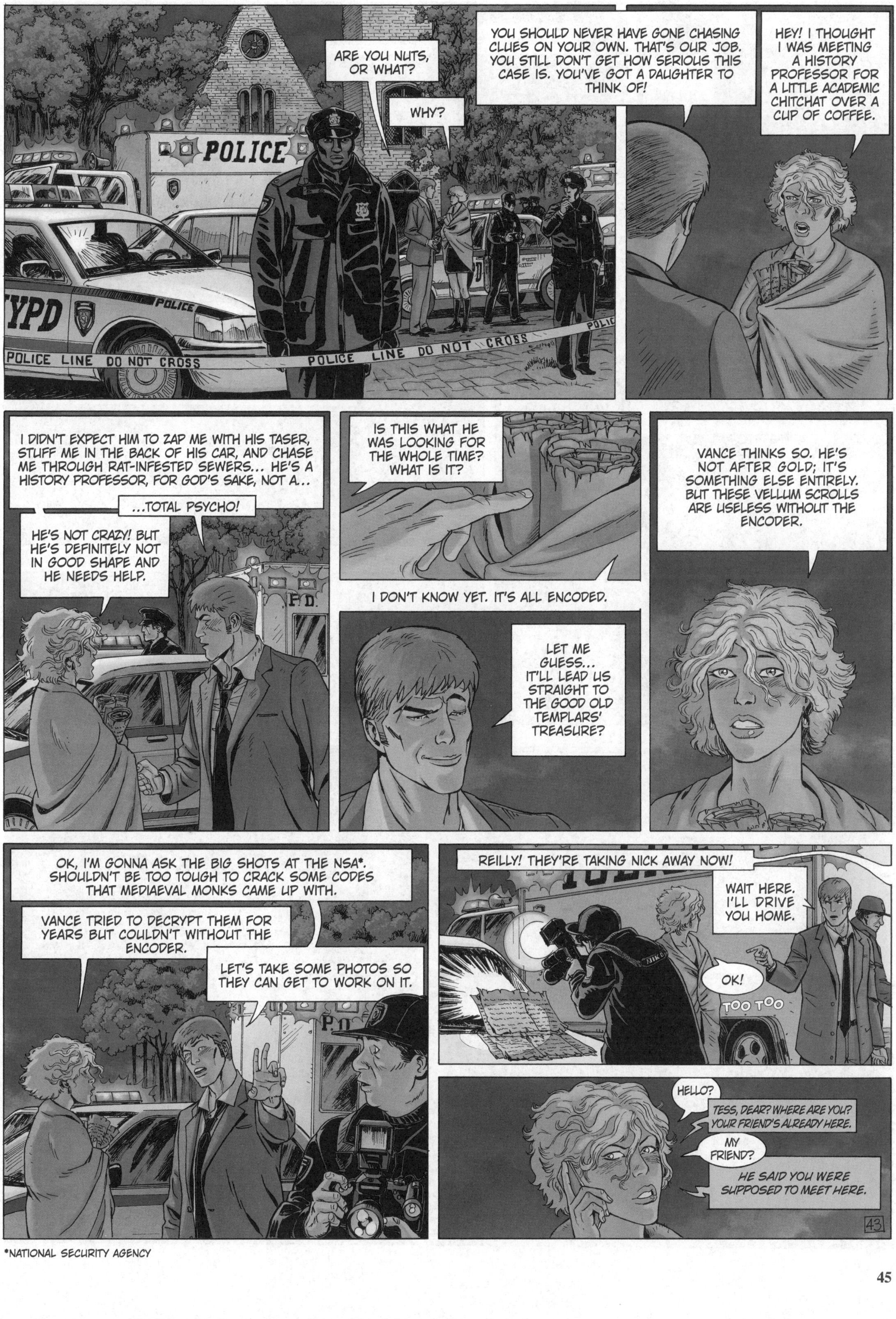

ARE YOU NUTS, OR WHAT?
WHY?
POLICE
NYPD
POLICE
POLICE LINE DO NOT CROSS
POLICE LINE DO NOT CROSS
YOU SHOULD NEVER HAVE GONE CHASING CLUES ON YOUR OWN. THAT'S OUR JOB. YOU STILL DON'T GET HOW SERIOUS THIS CASE IS. YOU'VE GOT A DAUGHTER TO THINK OF!
HEY! I THOUGHT I WAS MEETING A HISTORY PROFESSOR FOR A LITTLE ACADEMIC CHITCHAT OVER A CUP OF COFFEE.
I DIDN'T EXPECT HIM TO ZAP ME WITH HIS TASER, STUFF ME IN THE BACK OF HIS CAR, AND CHASE ME THROUGH RAT-INFESTED SEWERS... HE'S A HISTORY PROFESSOR, FOR GOD'S SAKE, NOT A...
...TOTAL PSYCHO!
HE'S NOT CRAZY! BUT HE'S DEFINITELY NOT IN GOOD SHAPE AND HE NEEDS HELP.
IS THIS WHAT HE WAS LOOKING FOR THE WHOLE TIME? WHAT IS IT?
I DON'T KNOW YET. IT'S ALL ENCODED.
LET ME GUESS... IT'LL LEAD US STRAIGHT TO THE GOOD OLD TEMPLARS' TREASURE?
VANCE THINKS SO. HE'S NOT AFTER GOLD; IT'S SOMETHING ELSE ENTIRELY. BUT THESE VELLUM SCROLLS ARE USELESS WITHOUT THE ENCODER.
OK, I'M GONNA ASK THE BIG SHOTS AT THE NSA*. SHOULDN'T BE TOO TOUGH TO CRACK SOME CODES THAT MEDIAEVAL MONKS CAME UP WITH.
VANCE TRIED TO DECRYPT THEM FOR YEARS BUT COULDN'T WITHOUT THE ENCODER.
LET'S TAKE SOME PHOTOS SO THEY CAN GET TO WORK ON IT.
REILLY! THEY'RE TAKING NICK AWAY NOW!
WAIT HERE. I'LL DRIVE YOU HOME.
OK!
TOO TOO
HELLO?
TESS, DEAR? WHERE ARE YOU? YOUR FRIEND'S ALREADY HERE.
MY FRIEND?
HE SAID YOU WERE SUPPOSED TO MEET HERE.
43

*NATIONAL SECURITY AGENCY

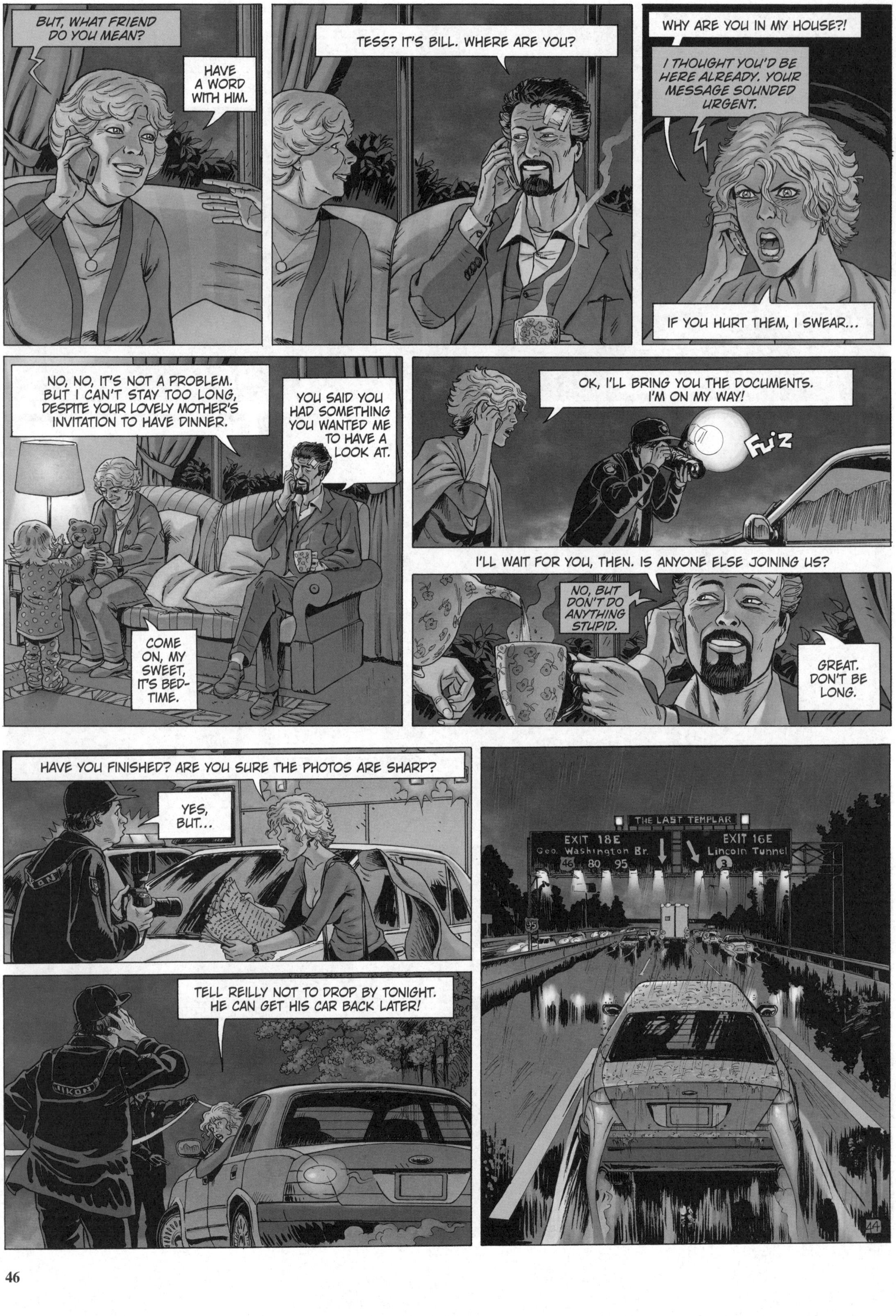

BUT, WHAT FRIEND DO YOU MEAN?
HAVE A WORD WITH HIM.
TESS? IT'S BILL. WHERE ARE YOU?
WHY ARE YOU IN MY HOUSE?!
I THOUGHT YOU'D BE HERE ALREADY. YOUR MESSAGE SOUNDED URGENT.
IF YOU HURT THEM, I SWEAR...
NO, NO, IT'S NOT A PROBLEM. BUT I CAN'T STAY TOO LONG, DESPITE YOUR LOVELY MOTHER'S INVITATION TO HAVE DINNER.
YOU SAID YOU HAD SOMETHING YOU WANTED ME TO HAVE A LOOK AT.
COME ON, MY SWEET, IT'S BED-TIME.
OK, I'LL BRING YOU THE DOCUMENTS. I'M ON MY WAY!
FLIZ
I'LL WAIT FOR YOU, THEN. IS ANYONE ELSE JOINING US?
NO, BUT DON'T DO ANYTHING STUPID.
GREAT. DON'T BE LONG.
HAVE YOU FINISHED? ARE YOU SURE THE PHOTOS ARE SHARP?
YES, BUT...
TELL REILLY NOT TO DROP BY TONIGHT. HE CAN GET HIS CAR BACK LATER!
THE LAST TEMPLAR
EXIT 18E
Geo. Washington Br.
46 80 95
EXIT 16E
Lincoln Tunnel
3
95
44

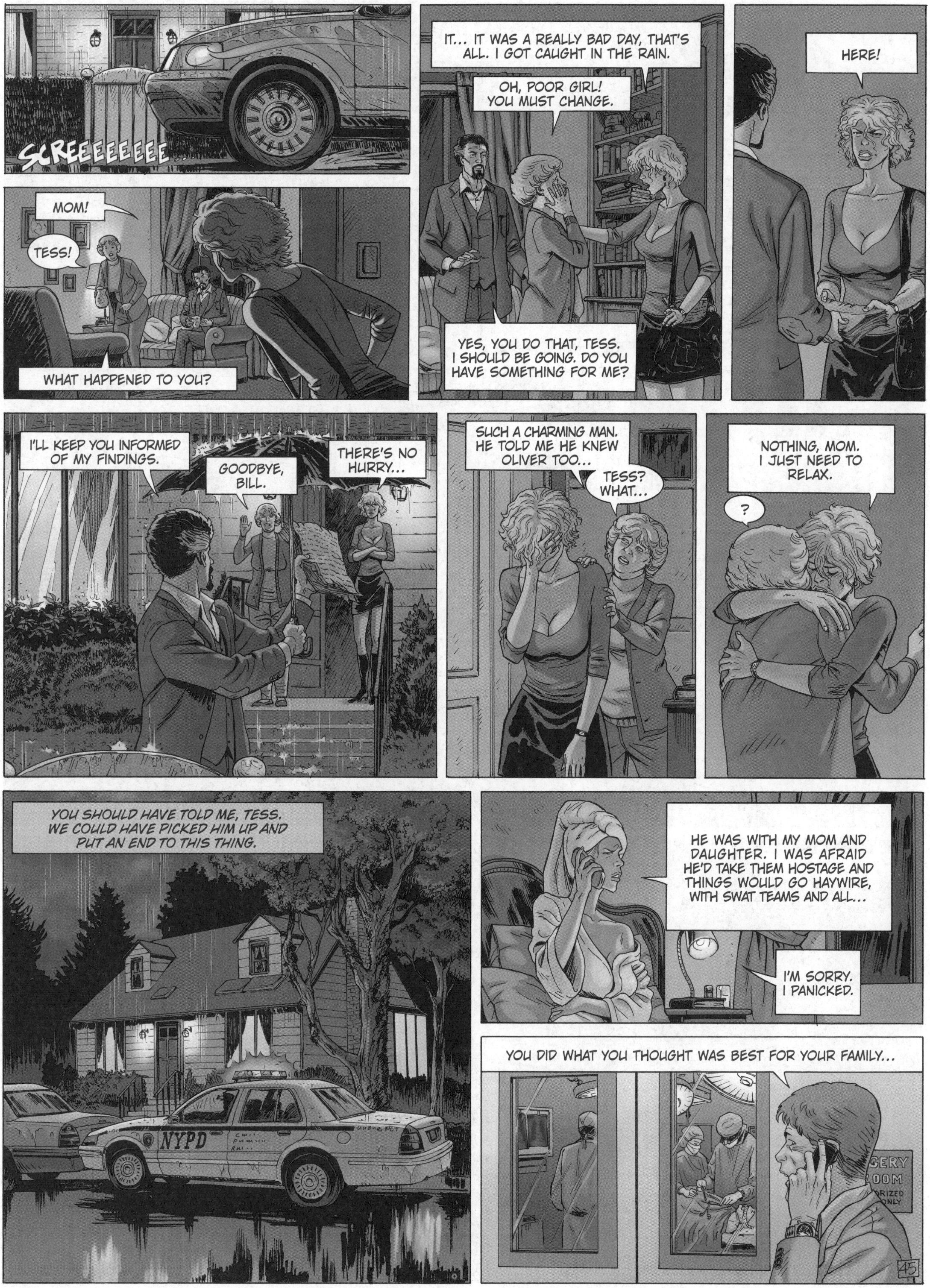
SCREEEEEEEE
MOM!
TESS!
WHAT HAPPENED TO YOU?
IT... IT WAS A REALLY BAD DAY, THAT'S ALL. I GOT CAUGHT IN THE RAIN.
OH, POOR GIRL! YOU MUST CHANGE.
YES, YOU DO THAT, TESS. I SHOULD BE GOING. DO YOU HAVE SOMETHING FOR ME?
HERE!
I'LL KEEP YOU INFORMED OF MY FINDINGS.
GOODBYE, BILL.
THERE'S NO HURRY...
SUCH A CHARMING MAN. HE TOLD ME HE KNEW OLIVER TOO...
TESS? WHAT...
NOTHING, MOM. I JUST NEED TO RELAX.
?
YOU SHOULD HAVE TOLD ME, TESS. WE COULD HAVE PICKED HIM UP AND PUT AN END TO THIS THING.
NYPD
HE WAS WITH MY MOM AND DAUGHTER. I WAS AFRAID HE'D TAKE THEM HOSTAGE AND THINGS WOULD GO HAYWIRE, WITH SWAT TEAMS AND ALL...
I'M SORRY. I PANICKED.
YOU DID WHAT YOU THOUGHT WAS BEST FOR YOUR FAMILY...
45

THANKS, SEAN. WHAT'S THE NSA SAYING?

IT'S TOO EARLY TO TELL, BUT THEIR FIRST IMPRESSION IS THAT DECODING THE MANUSCRIPT WON'T BE EASY. THEY DON'T HAVE ENOUGH TEXT TO BREAK THE EN-CRYPTION CODE.

HE HAS THE ENCODER AND THE PAPERS. ONCE HE'S DECODED THEM, HE'LL LEAVE FOR GOOD, YOU UNDERSTAND? WHATEVER HIS QUEST IS, IT'LL BE THOUSANDS OF MILES AWAY FROM HERE.

IF ONLY WE KNEW MORE ABOUT HOW THE ENCODER WORKS...

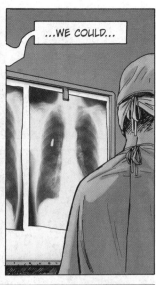

...WE COULD...

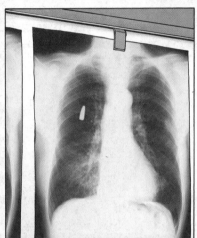

CALL ME AS SOON AS NICK'S OPERATION IS OVER!

SURGERY ROOM

BUCHINSKI, I'M TAKING YOUR CAR!

BUT...

YEEOOYEEOO

VVRRROOOOM

JFK AIRPORT...

YEEOOYEEOO...

HERE ARE ALL THE X-RAYS OF THE VATICAN SHIPMENT. IT WAS A HUGE CONVOY.

FREIGHT AND CARGO

ZOOM THROUGH THE IMAGES. I'LL LET YOU KNOW WHEN WE GET A HIT.

HOLD IT!

46

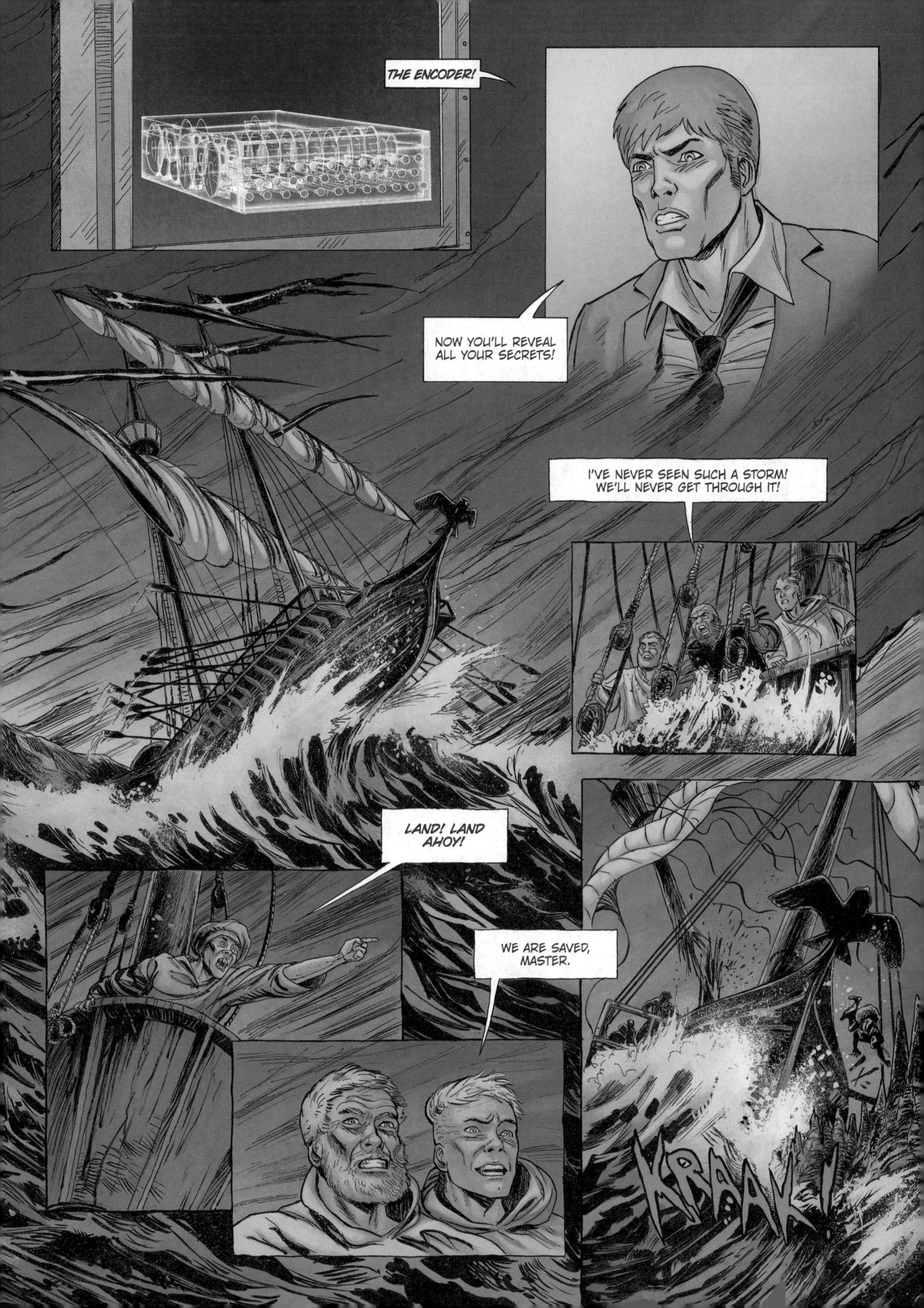
THE ENCODER!
NOW YOU'LL REVEAL ALL YOUR SECRETS!
I'VE NEVER SEEN SUCH A STORM! WE'LL NEVER GET THROUGH IT!
LAND! LAND AHOY!
WE ARE SAVED, MASTER.
KRAAK!

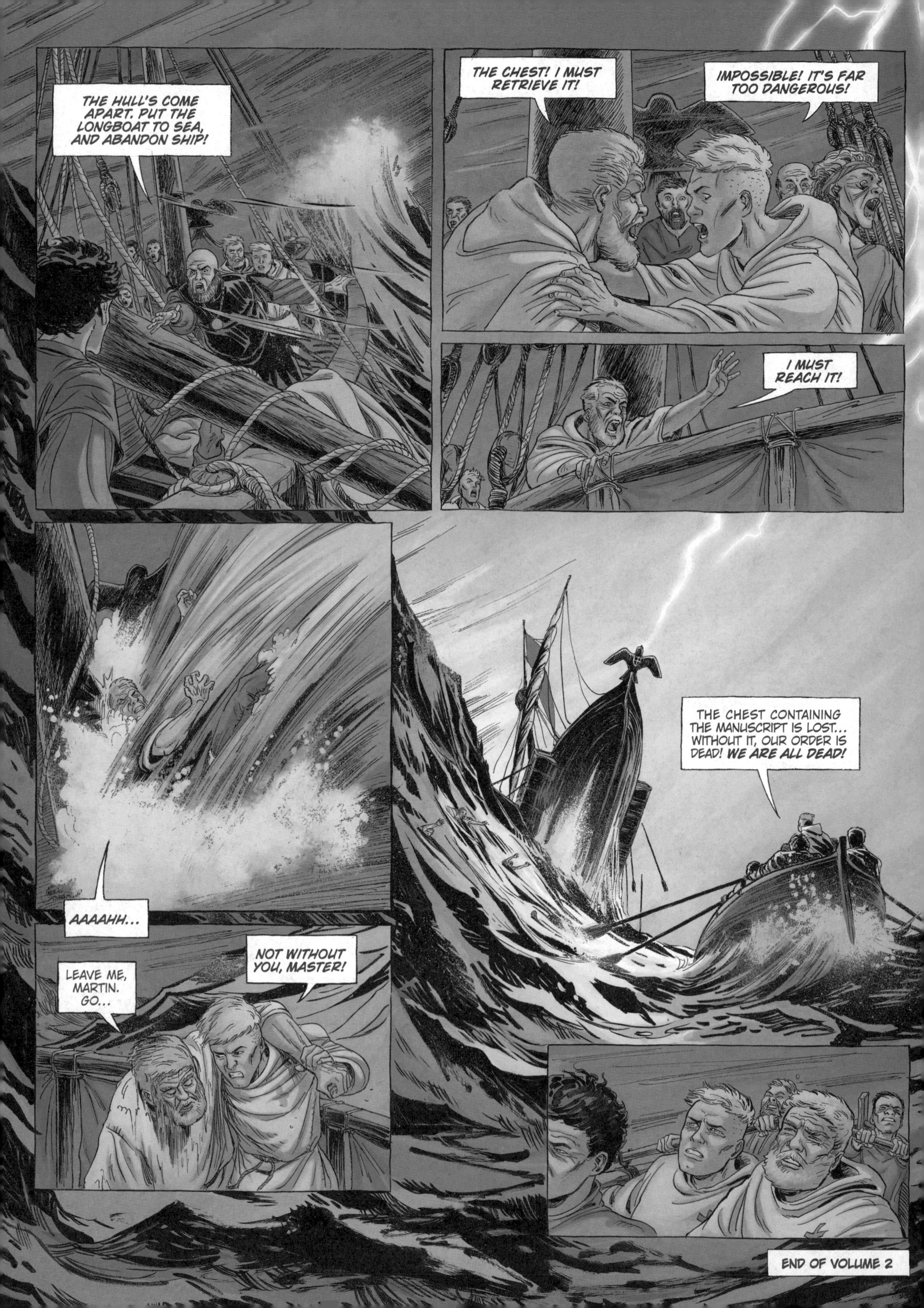
THE HULL'S COME APART. PUT THE LONGBOAT TO SEA, AND ABANDON SHIP!
THE CHEST! I MUST RETRIEVE IT!
IMPOSSIBLE! IT'S FAR TOO DANGEROUS!
I MUST REACH IT!
AAAAHH...
THE CHEST CONTAINING THE MANUSCRIPT IS LOST... WITHOUT IT, OUR ORDER IS DEAD! WE ARE ALL DEAD!
LEAVE ME, MARTIN. GO...
NOT WITHOUT YOU, MASTER!
END OF VOLUME 2

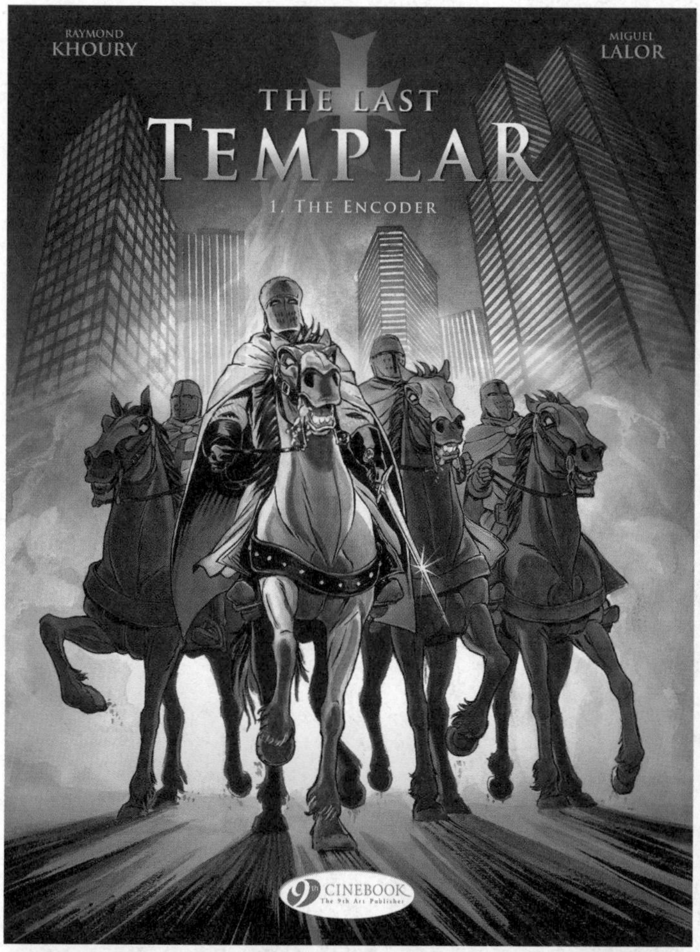
RAYMOND
KHOURY
MIGUEL
LALOR
THE LAST
TEMPLAR
1. The Encoder
CINEBOOK
The 9th Art Publisher

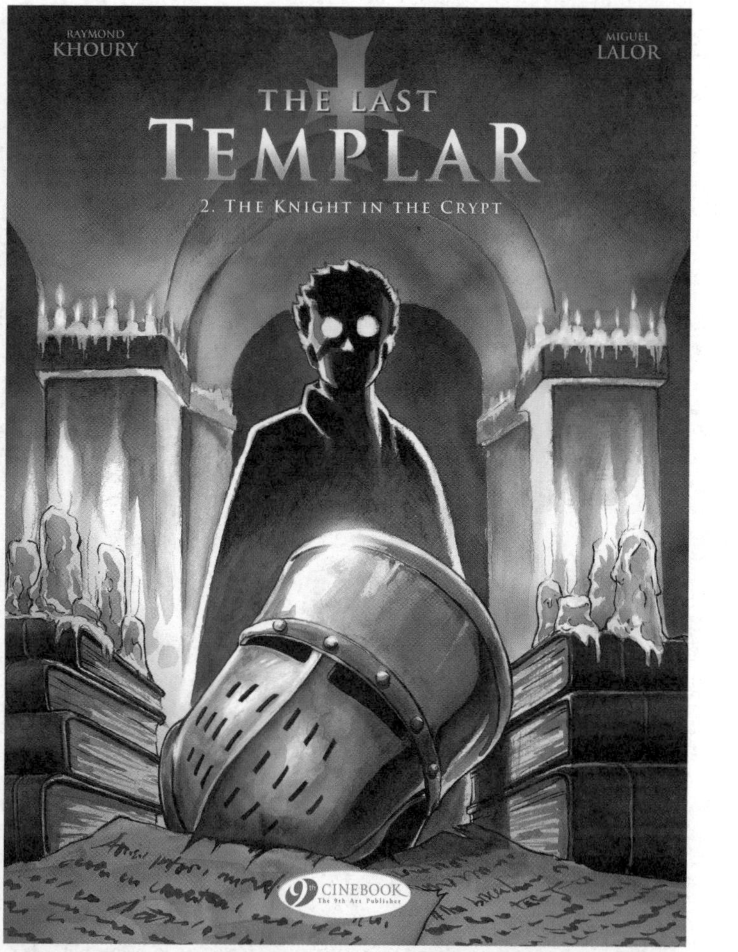
RAYMOND
KHOURY
MIGUEL
LALOR
THE LAST
TEMPLAR
2. The Knight in the Crypt
CINEBOOK
The 9th Art Publisher

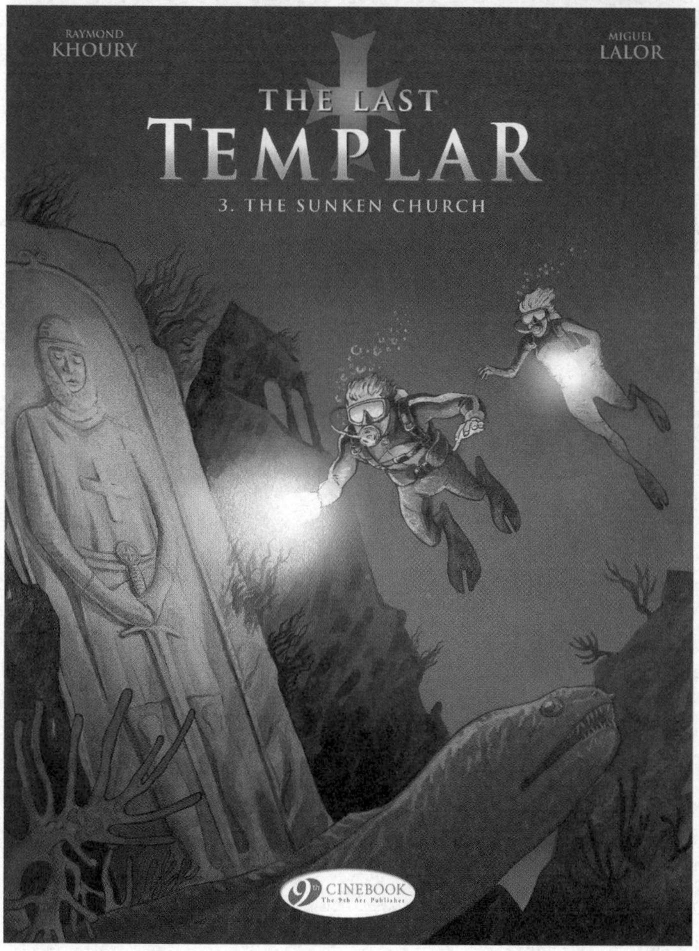
RAYMOND
KHOURY
MIGUEL
LALOR
THE LAST
TEMPLAR
3. THE SUNKEN CHURCH
CINEBOOK
The 9th Art Publisher

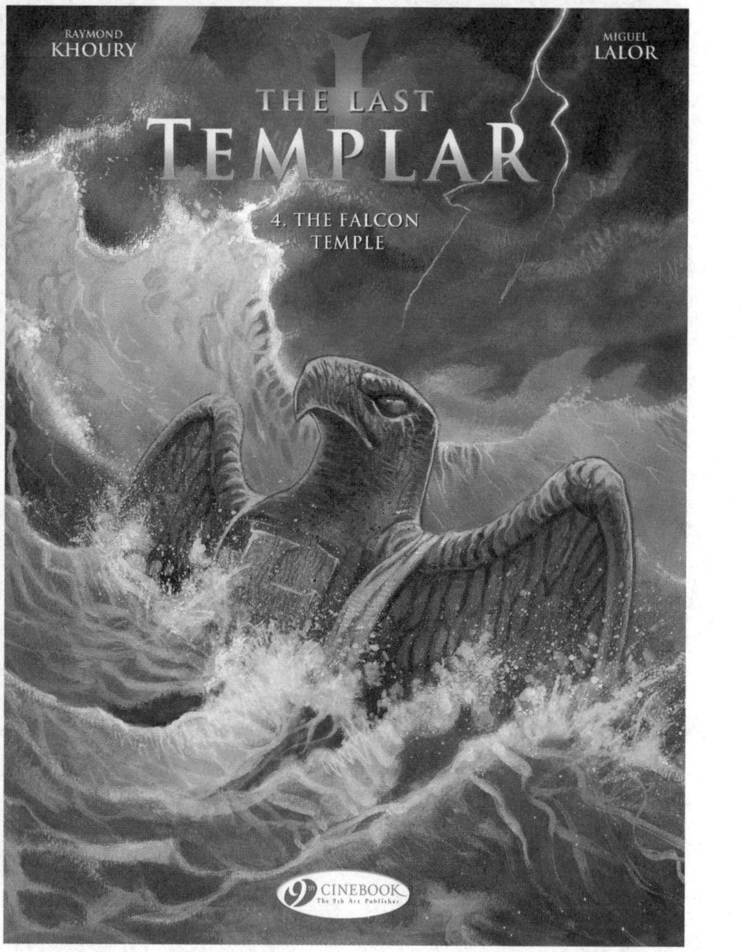
RAYMOND
KHOURY
MIGUEL
LALOR
THE LAST
TEMPLAR
4. THE FALCON
TEMPLE
CINEBOOK
The 9th Art Publisher

COMING SOON

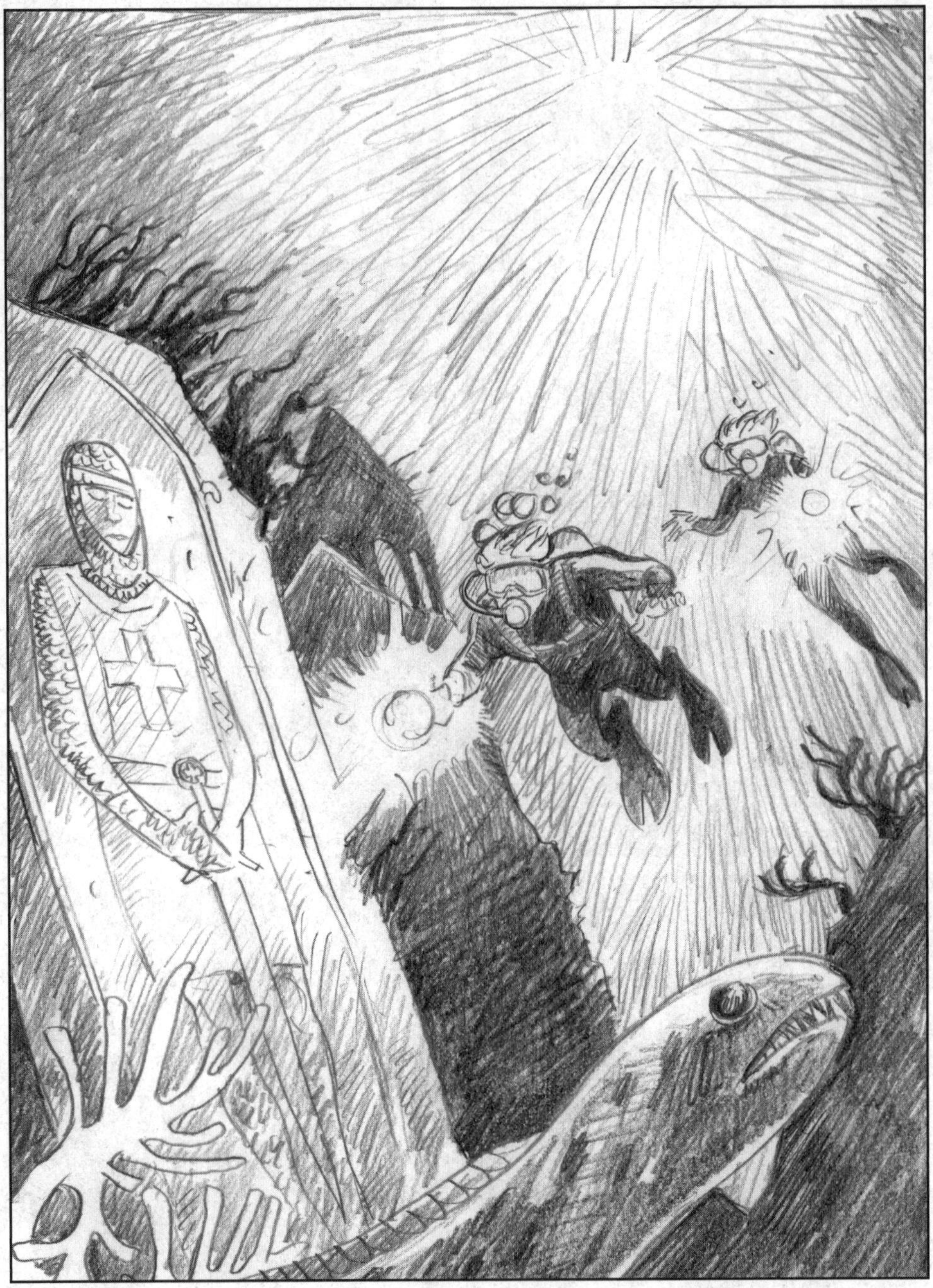

THE SUNKEN CHURCH

It's off to Turkey for Tess and Sean – and their mysterious pursuers.

After being kidnapped by Vance and subsequently escaping, Tess is now officially part of the investigative team alongside Agent Reilly. But despite the constant danger of the lurking assassins who have already nearly killed her once, the young woman refuses to play a passive role. Her research will take her far from New York, under the protection of Sean Reilly – who is about to face a terrible crisis of faith.

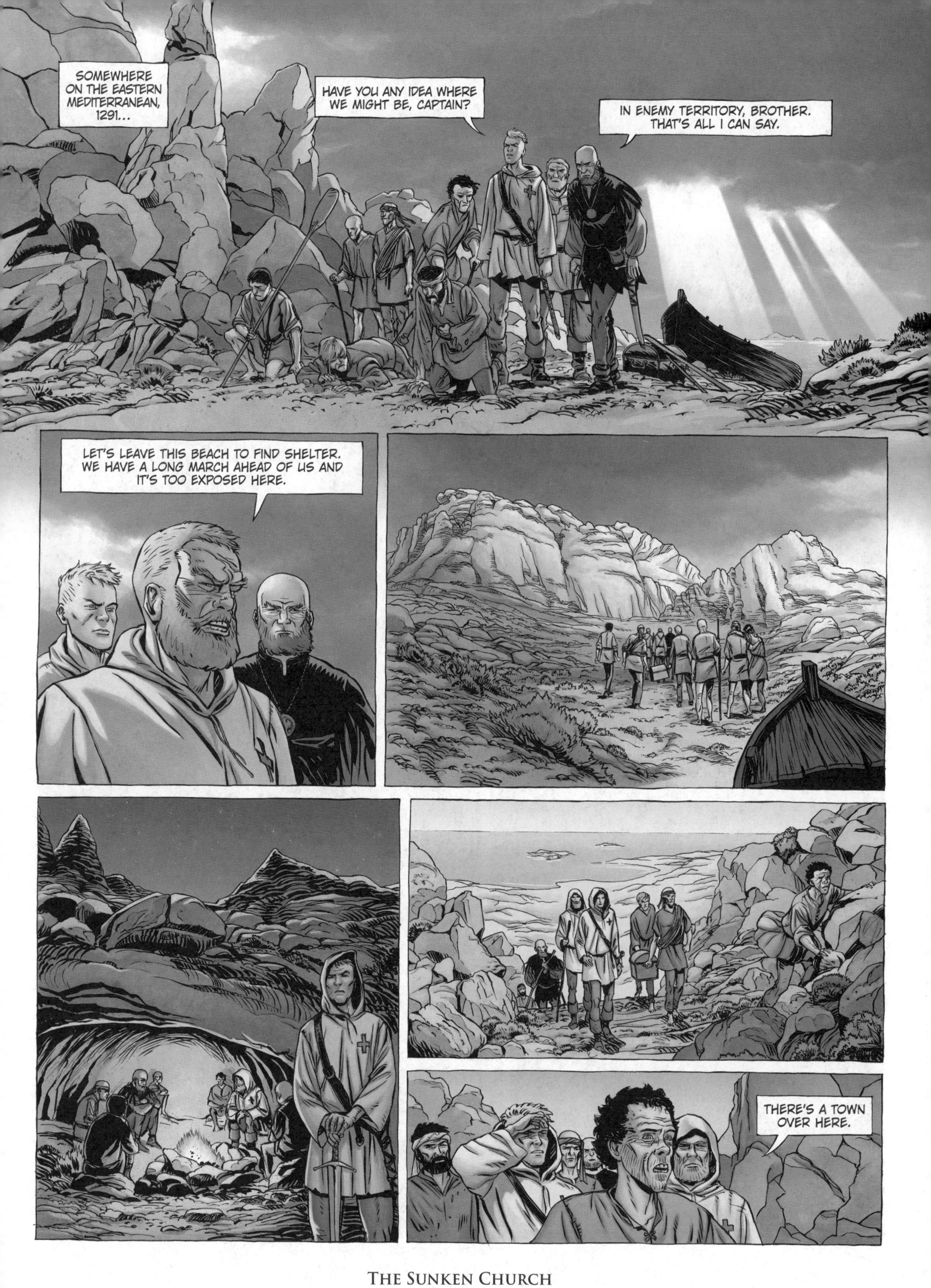
SOMEWHERE ON THE EASTERN MEDITERRANEAN, 1291...
HAVE YOU ANY IDEA WHERE WE MIGHT BE, CAPTAIN?
IN ENEMY TERRITORY, BROTHER. THAT'S ALL I CAN SAY.
LET'S LEAVE THIS BEACH TO FIND SHELTER. WE HAVE A LONG MARCH AHEAD OF US AND IT'S TOO EXPOSED HERE.
THERE'S A TOWN OVER HERE.

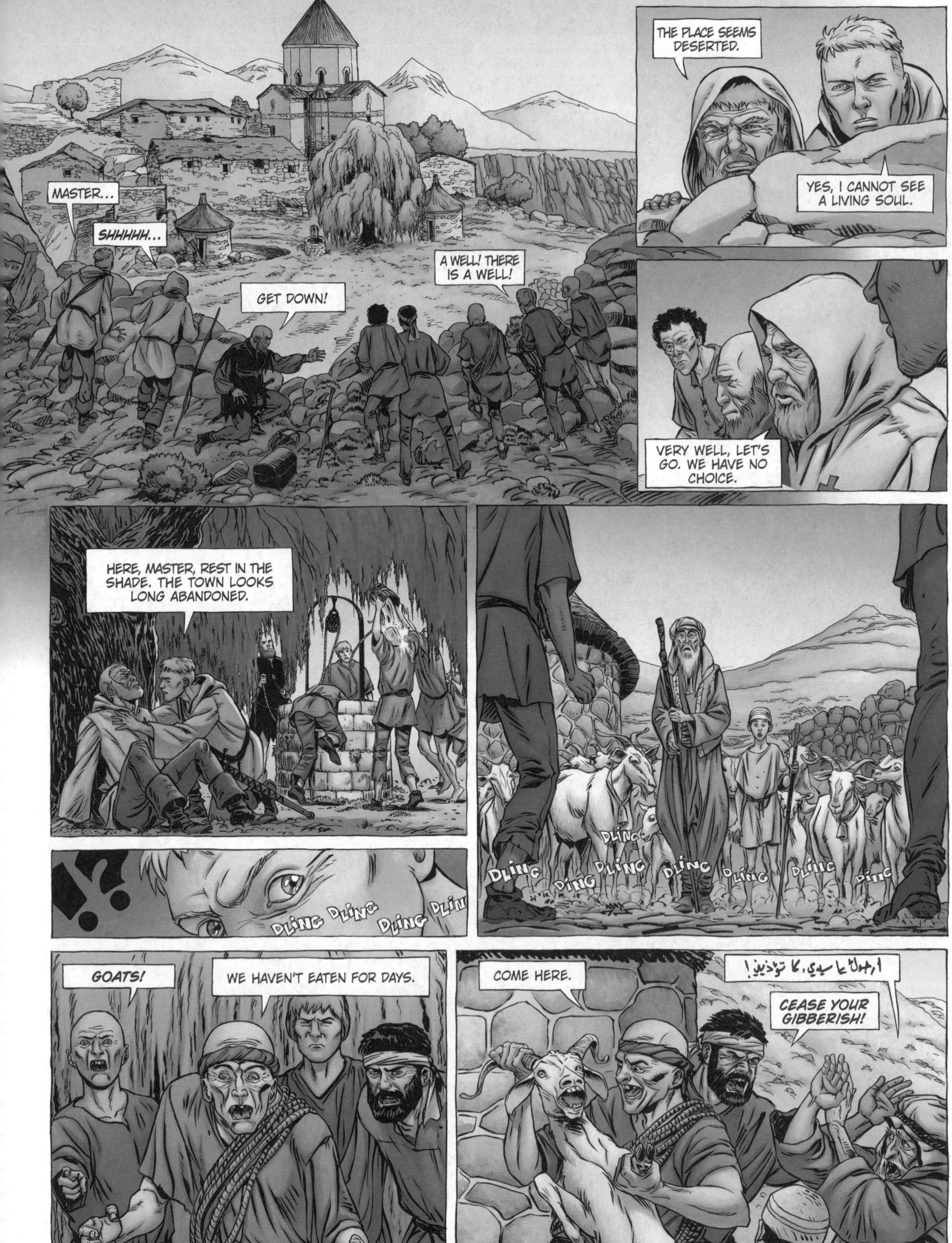
MASTER...
SHHHHH...
GET DOWN!
A WELL! THERE IS A WELL!
THE PLACE SEEMS DESERTED.
YES, I CANNOT SEE A LIVING SOUL.
VERY WELL, LET'S GO. WE HAVE NO CHOICE.
HERE, MASTER, REST IN THE SHADE. THE TOWN LOOKS LONG ABANDONED.
!?
DLING DLING DLING DLIN
DLING DING DLING DLING DLING DLING DING DLING
GOATS!
WE HAVEN'T EATEN FOR DAYS.
COME HERE.
ارجوك يا سيدي، لا تؤذيني!
CEASE YOUR GIBBERISH!
2

*PLEASE, SIRE, DO NOT HURT US!

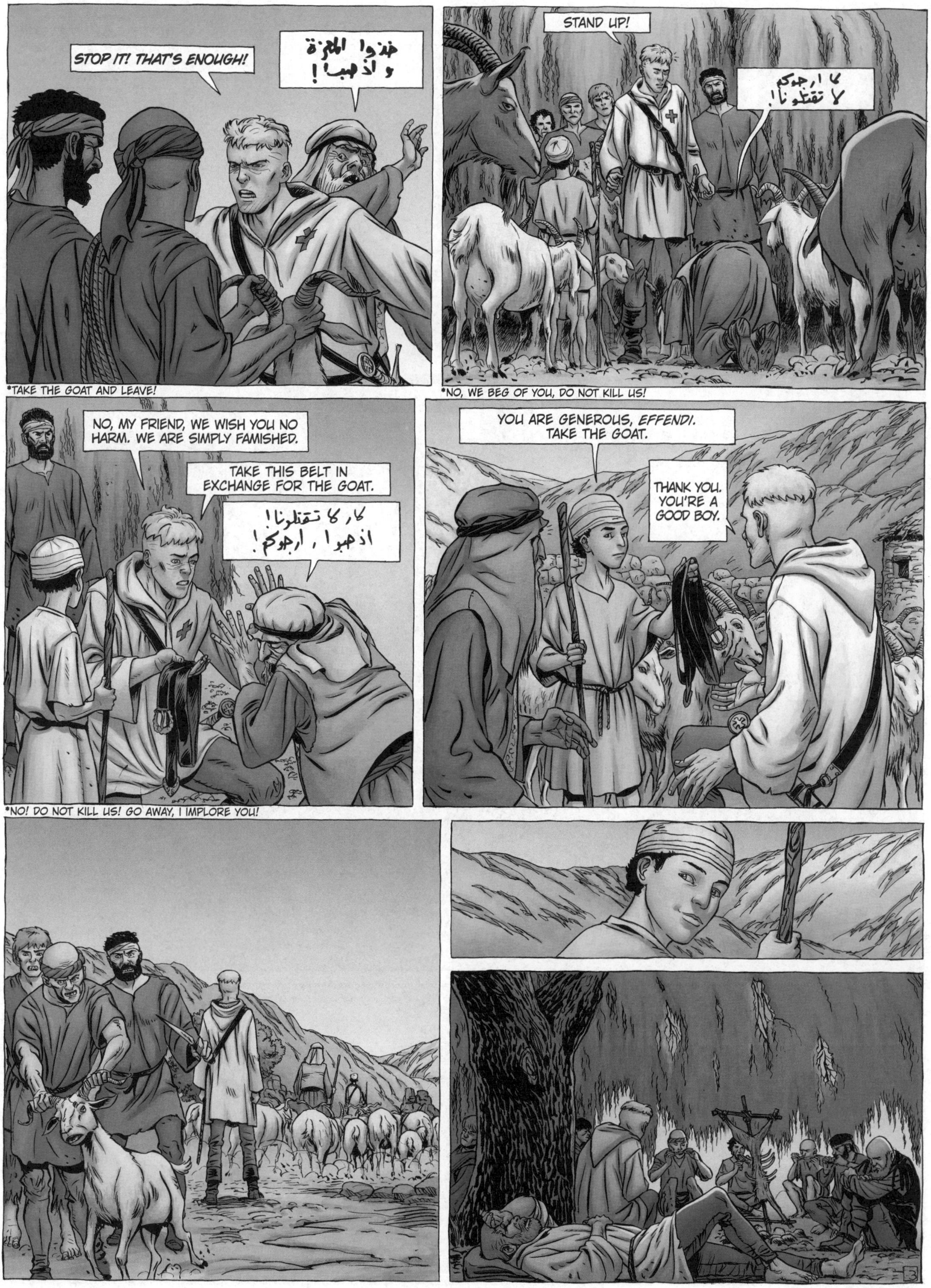

STOP IT! THAT'S ENOUGH!
خذوا المعزة و اذهبوا !
*TAKE THE GOAT AND LEAVE!
STAND UP!
لا ارجوكم لا تقتلونا !
*NO, WE BEG OF YOU, DO NOT KILL US!
NO, MY FRIEND, WE WISH YOU NO HARM. WE ARE SIMPLY FAMISHED.
TAKE THIS BELT IN EXCHANGE FOR THE GOAT.
لا، لا تقتلونا ! اذهبوا ، ارجوكم !
*NO! DO NOT KILL US! GO AWAY, I IMPLORE YOU!
YOU ARE GENEROUS, *EFFENDI*. TAKE THE GOAT.
THANK YOU. YOU'RE A GOOD BOY.

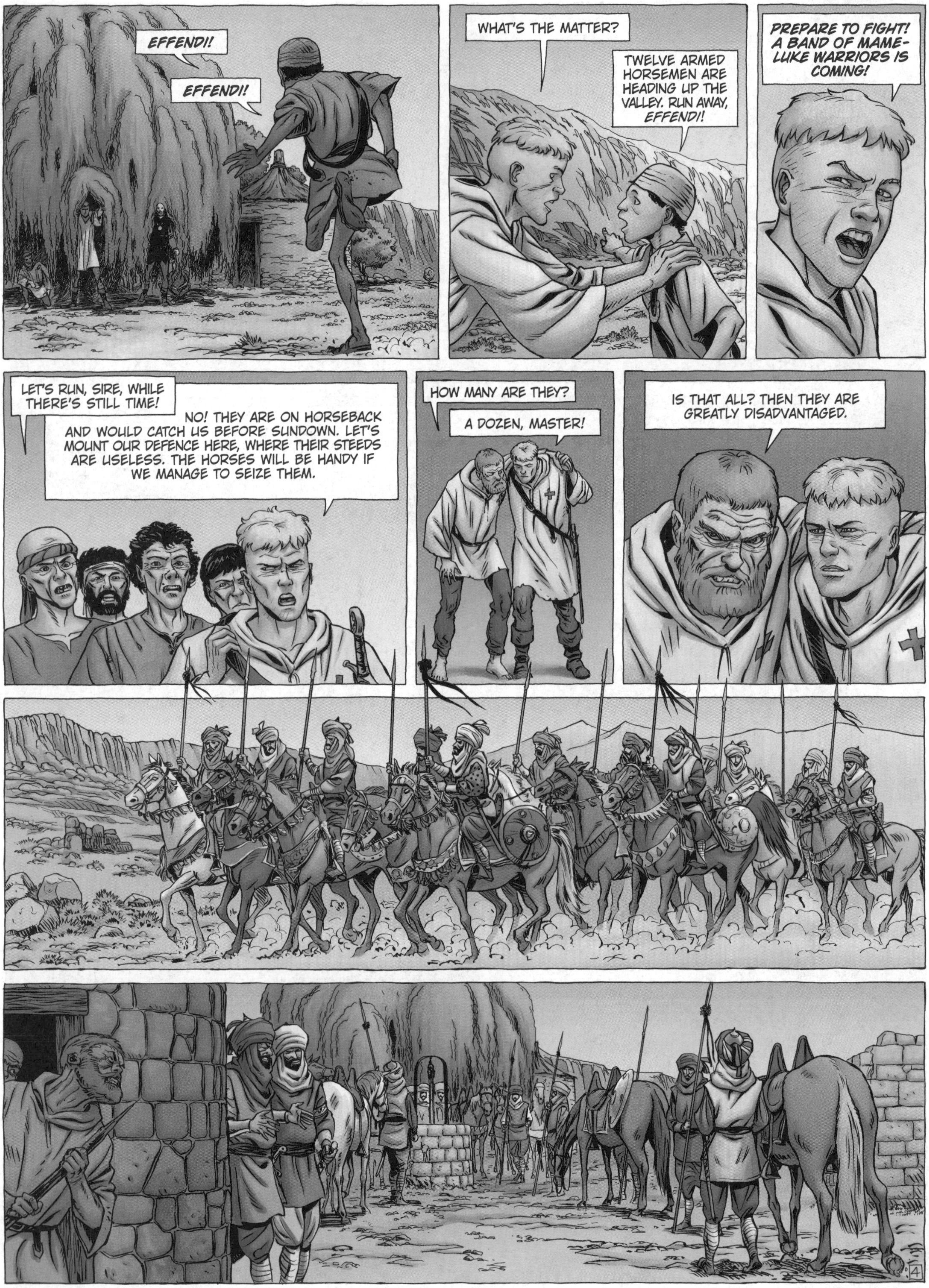

EFFENDI!
EFFENDI!
WHAT'S THE MATTER?
TWELVE ARMED HORSEMEN ARE HEADING UP THE VALLEY. RUN AWAY, EFFENDI!
PREPARE TO FIGHT! A BAND OF MAME-LUKE WARRIORS IS COMING!
LET'S RUN, SIRE, WHILE THERE'S STILL TIME!
NO! THEY ARE ON HORSEBACK AND WOULD CATCH US BEFORE SUNDOWN. LET'S MOUNT OUR DEFENCE HERE, WHERE THEIR STEEDS ARE USELESS. THE HORSES WILL BE HANDY IF WE MANAGE TO SEIZE THEM.
HOW MANY ARE THEY?
A DOZEN, MASTER!
IS THAT ALL? THEN THEY ARE GREATLY DISADVANTAGED.
4